YORUBA CULTURE

Table of Contents

Abiku 1
Adire (textile art) 1
Aláàrìnjó 2
Ayagunna 2
Ayoayo 2
Babalawo 3
Death and the King's Horseman 4
Egungun 8
Epa mask 9
Ibeji 10
Ifá 11
Itutu 15
Obaala 16
Ọba kò so 16
Oduduwa 16
Oríkì 18
Orisha 18
Ori (Yoruba) 20
The Lion and the Jewel 21
The Strong Breed 24
Yoruba Academy 24
Yoruba culture 24
Yoruba language 27
Yoruba literature 30
Yoruba medicine 31
Yoruba music 34
Yoruba name 36
Yoruba religion 36
Yoruba traditional art 39
Article summaries 40

Preface

Each chapter in this book ends with a URL to a hyperlinked online version. Use the online version to access related pages, websites, footnotes, color photos, updates, copyright, or to see the chapter's contributors. Click the edit link to suggest changes.

In the last chapter we have computer-selected article summaries that mention topics in the book. We ask online booksellers to include a list of articles in the book's description.

Most summaries include a URL to the full text version of the article. Please type the URL exactly as it appears. If you change the URL's capitalization, for example, it may not work. You may find multiple listings for articles available from different URLs. If there's no URL, simply search Google or your local library's website on the article's title to get the URL.

Purchase of this book entitles you to a free trial membership in the publisher's book club at www.university-press.org. (Time limited offer.) Simply enter the barcode number from the back cover or to the membership form on our home page. The book club entitles you to select from millions of books at no additional charge, including a PDF copy of this and related books to read on the go. Simply enter the title or subject onto the search form to find them.

If you have any questions, could you please be so kind as to consult our Frequently Asked Questions page at www.university-press.org/faqs.cfm? You are also welcome to contact us there.

Publisher: University Press, Books LLC, Memphis, TN, USA, 2012.

Abiku

Abiku is a word in Yoruba. The word is derived from Yoruba: (abiku) "predestined to death", which is from (abi) "that which possesses" and (iku) "death". Abiku refers to the spirits of children who die before reaching puberty; a child who dies before twelve years of age being called an Abiku, and the spirit, or spirits, who caused the death being also called Abiku.

Ben Okri's novel *The Famished Road* is based upon an abiku. Debo Kotun's novel *Abiku*, a political satire of the Nigerian military oligarchy, is based upon an abiku. Gerald Brom's illustrated novel, *The Plucker*, depicts a child's toys fighting against an abiku.

Source http://en.wikipedia.org/wiki/Abiku

Adire (textile art)

Adire (Yoruba — tie and dye) textile is the indigo dyed cloth made in south western Nigeria by Yoruba women, using a variety of resist dye techniques.

As the translation of the name suggests, the earliest pieces of this type were probably simple tied designs on cotton cloth handspun and woven locally (rather like those still produced in Mali), but in the early decades of the 20th century new access to large quantities of imported shirting material via the spread of European textile merchants in Abeokuta and other Yoruba towns caused a boom in these women's entrepreneurial and artistic efforts, making adire a major local craft in Abeokuta and Ibadan, attracting buyers from all over West Africa. The cloth's basic shape became that of two pieces of shirting material stitched together to create a women's wrapper cloth.

New techniques of resist dyeing developed, such as "adire eleko" (hand-painting designs onto cloth with a cassava starch paste prior to dyeing), along with a new style more suited to rapid mass production (using metal stencils cut from the sheets of tin that lined tea chests, using sewn raffia and/or tied sections, or folding the cloths repeatedly before tying or stitching them in place). Most of the designs were named, with popular ones including the jubilee pattern, (first produced for the silver jubilee of George V and Queen Mary in

1935), Olokun ("goddess of the sea"), and Ibadadun ("Ibadan is sweet").

However, by the end of the 1930s the spread of synthetic indigo and caustic soda and an influx of new less skilled entrants caused quality problems and a still-present collapse in demand. Though the more complex and beautiful starch resist designs continued to be produced until the early 1970s, but despite a revival prompted largely by the interest of US Peace Corps workers in the 1960s, never regained their earlier popularity. In the present day simplified stencilled designs and some better quality tie & die and stitch-resist designs are still produced, but local taste favours "kampala" (multi-coloured wax resist cloth, sometimes also known as adire by a few people).

Source http://en.wikipedia.org/wiki/Adire_(textile_art)

Aláàrìnjó

Aláàrìnjó is a traditional dance-theatre troupe among the Yoruba.

According to music historian Roger Blench, Aláàrìnjó dates back to the sixteenth century and probably developed from the Egúngún masquerade. However, it soon became professional and split into competing groups. Improved roads allowed groups to travel further and outdo other groups with special effects. The heart of these groups are traditional drums, but in modern performances these are being displaced by heavily amplified European instruments, recorded sound tracks and even short film extracts.

The Aláàrìnjó groups were also the inspiration for the 'African Music Research Party' founded by Chief Hubert Ogunde in 1946, the ancestor of modern professional theatre troupes.

Source http://en.wikipedia.org/wiki/Aláàrìnjó

Ayagunna

Ayagunna is the youngest path, or avatar, of the undergod Obatala in the Lukumi (Santería) pantheon. In this manifestation, Obatala is a youth who battles with a scimitar. He is credited with having spread gun powder throughout the world. In addition, he travelled to Asia, where he warred against and defeated his enemies, bringing their slain heads along with him as evidence of his destruction. The normally peaceful and calm Obatala manifests a fierceness and thirst for peace by way of domination in this aspect.

In the Lukumi system, Ayagunna can turn out to be one's governing orisha. His receptacle contains the requisite items of Obatala as well as additional ones that are designated only to that path. When one receives Ochanla, one must already be in possession of Ayagunna or receive him alongside with her. Although Obatala eats female animals due to his duality and age, after receiving Ochanla the adherent must now feed Ayagunna male animals and Ochanla female. Ayagunna is often envisioned in a similar fashion to Shango. He is a member of the fun-fun (white) court of Obatala as a divine king, as are all of his other manifestations. When his adherents manifest his energies during religious trance sessions, Ayagunna behaves with swift, strong, and battle like movements. Hence, he is the paladin among orishas. His children are often mistaken for children of Shango.

Ayagunna wears all white with the exception of a diagonal red sash that bisects his tunic. The *patakis* or stories of the faith state that Olofin put Ayagunna in charge of bringing order to the Earth since Man had been left to his own devices. At first, Ayagunna asked the people to bring their lives in line with the laws of Olofi but they ignored his requests. After a while, Ayagunna grew less and less patient and finally stopped making requests and took more punitive measures by executing those who refused to obey. Word got back to Olofi, and he travelled to our World from Ara Onu to see for himself what Ayagunna had wrought. When Ayagunna saw Olofi coming, he wiped his scimitar across his chest to clean the blood from its blade. Olofi scolded Ayagunna for causing such confusion, but Ayagunna then responded in a lawyerly fashion "Father without conflict, there can be no progress". Olofi considered his words and subsequently agreed.

Ayagunna is also known for being the breeder of conflict and war. His name literally means "war dog".

Ayagunna said the day he lays down his sword, the world will cease to exist.

Ayagunna is a Spanish mispronuciation of the proper Yoruba Ajaguna. In Spanish, the j sounds like a y.

Source http://en.wikipedia.org/wiki/Ayagunna

Ayoayo

Ayoayo is a traditional mancala played by the Yoruba people in Nigeria. It is very close to (and possibly a direct ancestor of) the Warri game that spread to the Americas with the atlantic slave trade. Among modern mancalas, which are most often derived from Warri, the Kalah is a notable one that has essentially the same rules as Ayoayo.

There are games with identical rules also in other areas of Africa. One such game is the Endodoi, played by the

Equipment and initial setup of the Ayoayo game

Maasai people of Kenya and Tanzania.

Rules

The Ayoayo board is composed of two roles of six holes each, and 48 seeds are used; at the beginning, 4 seeds are placed in each hole. These are exactly the same equipment and setup as those of Warri and many other 2-row mancalas such as Layli Goobalay. Each player own one of the rows.

At his or her turn, the player takes all seeds from one of his holes and relay sows them counterclockwise; during each individual sowing, the starting hole is skipped (i.e., no seeds are dropped there even if more than 12 seeds are to be sown). When the last seed is sown in an empty hole, and if this hole belongs to the player in turn, he or she will capture any seed in the opposing hole

When one of the players cannot move anymore, the game is over. The opponent captures all the seeds that are left on the board and the winner is the player who captured most seeds.

Notice that if a player ends his or her turn with no seeds left in his or her row, the opponent *must* (if it is possible) choose his move in such a way to bring one or more seeds into the other's row. This scheme is found in many mancalas and sometimes referred to as "feeding" the opponent (i.e., save the opponent from starving).

Source http://en.wikipedia.org/wiki/Ayoayo

Babalawo

Babalawo (Babaaláwo in full and pronounced Baba-a-láwo, literally meaning 'father or master of the mysticism' in the Yoruba language) is a Yorùbá chieftaincy title that denotes a Priest of Ifá. Ifa is a divination system that represents the teachings of the Orisha Orunmila, the Spirit of Wisdom, who in turn serves as the oracular representative of God. The Babalawo claim to ascertain the future through communication with Orunmila. This is done through the interpretation of either the patterns of the divining chain known as *Opele*, or the palm nuts called *Ikin*, on the traditionally wooden divination tray.

The Awo in a Yoruba community

Awo undergo training in the memorization and interpretation of the 256 *Odu* or mysteries, as well as in the numerous verses or *Ese* of Ifa. Traditionally, the Babalawo usually have additional professional specialities. For instance, several would also be herbalists, while others would specialize in extinguishing the troubles caused by Ajogun. The Babalawo are, however, generally trained in the determination of problems and the application of both spiritual and related secular solutions to these problems. Their primary function is to assist people in finding, understanding and processing the vagaries of life until they experience spiritual wisdom as a part of their daily experience. The Awo is charged with helping people develop the discipline and character that supports such spiritual growth. This is done by identifying the client's spiritual destiny, or Ori, and developing a spiritual blueprint which can be used to support, cultivate and live out that destiny.

Because spiritual development of others is the charge of Awo, they must dedicate themselves to improving their own understanding of life and be proper examples for others. The Awo that does not hold his own behavior to the highest moral standards will fall out of favor with his or her Orisa community, thus creating a saituation where he will be judged more harshly than others would be for like transgressions.

Some Awo are initiated as adolescents, while others learn as full adults. In either case, training and years of dedication are still the hallmark of the most learned and spiritually gifted Awos. This is why on average, most Ifa initiates train for as long as a decade before they are recognized as "complete" Babalawos.

The Iyanifa

Ifa priestesses are called Iyanifa. Awo is often used as a gender-neutral reference to individual Iyanifa or Babalawo, as well as to the group as a whole. An Awo is a spiritual counsellor to clients and those whom he or she may have assisted in receiving tutelary Orisa shrines and/or initiation into the spiritual tradition of the Orisa.

On the other hand, in Cuba and parts of Nigeria such as Ode Remo,Ijebuland and Ibadan, the position of the Iyanifa as a divining priestess of Ifa is hotly contested on the grounds that in the Ifa Odus Ogunda Ka and Oshe Yekun, no one can become a full Awo Ifa without the presence of Odun, and in the Odu Ifa Irete Ntelu (Irete Ogbe), Odun herself says that she would only marry Orunmila if he promised not to permit women to be in the same room as her. These views appear to be confirmed by books published in Nigeria as far back as the 19th century. For instance, the eminent Yoruba author James Johnson wrote in one of the most detailed early descriptions of Ifa that "Whenever this should be the case, a woman would receive from a Babalawo only one Ikin or Consecrated Palm nut called Eko, which she would carry about her body for her protection, and whenever divination should recommend and prescribe to her sacrifice to Ifa, she would, for the time being, hand over her Eko either to her husband or to her brother, or any other male relative according to prescription, who would include it in his own Ikins for the purpose of the worship and sacrifice in which she would participate." William Bascom, the foremost academic authority on Ifa up until the time of his death, also stated that "only men can become babalawo" and that he never encountered a single female Ifa priest acting as a diviner during any of his extensive field studies in the cities of Ife, Igana, Meko, Oyo, Ilesa, Abeokuta, Osogbo, Sagamu, Ilara, Ondo, Ijebu Ode or Ekiti in Yorubaland in 1937-38, 1950–51, in 1960 and 1965, nor did any of his informants mention such a thing. Sources from Yorubaland going back to the mid-19th century clearly state that only men can become Ifa diviners.

Resources

Fagbemijo Amosun Fakayode, *All Days Are Sacred* 2011 All Days Are Sacred
Charles Spencer King, *Nature's Ancient Religion* ISBN 978-1-4404-1733-7
Chief S. Solagbade Popoola & Fakunle Oyesanya, Ikunle Abiyamo: The ASE of Motherhood 2007. ISBN 978-0-9810013-0-2
Chief S. Solagbade Popoola Library, INC Ifa Dida Volume One (EjiOgbe - Orangun Meji) ISBN 978-0-9810013-1-9 Chief S. Solagbade Popoola Library, INC Ifa Dida Volume Two (OgbeYeku - OgbeFun) ISBN Chief S. Solagbade Popoola Library, INC Ifa Dida Volume Three (OyekuOgbe - OyekuFun) ISBN

Notes and references

Source http://en.wikipedia.org/wiki/Babalawo

Death and the King's Horseman

Death and the King's Horseman	
Written by	Wole Soyinka
Characters	Elesin
	Olunde
	Iyaloja
	Simon Pilkings
	Jane Pilkings
	Amusa
Date premiered	March 1, 1975
Place premiered	Vivian Beaumont Theatre
Original language	English
Setting	Nigeria, 1944

Death and the King's Horseman is a play by Wole Soyinka based on a real incident that took place in Nigeria during British colonial rule: the ritual suicide of the horseman of an important chief was prevented by the intervention of the colonial authorities. In addition to the British intervention, Soyinka calls the horseman's own conviction toward suicide into question, posing a problem that throws off the community's balance.

Plot

Death and The King's Horseman builds upon the true story to focus on the character of Elesin, the King's Horseman of the title. According to a Yoruba tradition, the death of a chief must be followed by the ritual suicide of the chief's horseman, because the horseman's spirit is essential to helping the chief's spirit ascend to the afterlife. Otherwise, the chief's spirit will wander the earth and bring harm to the Yoruba people. The first half of the play documents the process of this ritual, with the potent, life-loving figure Elesin living out his final day in celebration before the ritual process begins. At the last minute the local British colonial ruler, Simon Pilkings, intervenes, the suicide being viewed as barbaric and illegal by the British authorities.

In the play, the result for the community is catastrophic, as the breaking of the ritual means the disruption of the cosmic order of the universe and thus the well-being and future of the collectivity is in doubt. As the action unfolds, the community blames Elesin as much as Pilkings, accusing him of being too attached to the earth to fulfill his spiritual obligations. Events lead to tragedy when Elesin's son, Olunde, who has returned to Nigeria from studying medicine in Europe, takes on the responsibility of his father and commits ritual suicide in his place so as to restore the honour of his family and the order of the universe. Consequently, Elesin kills himself, condemning his soul to a degraded existence in the next world. In addition, the dialogue of the native suggests that this may have been insufficient and that the world is now "adrift in the void".

Another Nigerian playwright, Duro Ladipo, had already written a play in the Yoruba language based on this incident, called *Oba waja* (*The King is Dead*).

Yoruba Perception of the World Around Them

The way in which the Yoruba peoples view the world must be understood before *Death and the King's Horseman* can be accurately interpreted. Yoruba culture has several key ideas that are presented using language, imagery, and different behaviors. Thinking like a Yoruba individual requires that these three mediums be experienced, internalized and visualized within the "mind's eye". When one experiences any one of these methods of expression, what is perceived within the mind, namely the *iran* ("mental image") becomes closely linked to the perceiver's *oju inu* ("inner eye" or "insight"). Experiencing words, images, and behaviors, the Yoruba believe, results in the interaction of two key Yoruba concepts, that of the *iran* and of the *oju inu*, the interaction of which is like a fusion—when the *iran* is perceived by the *oju inu*, it is as if that image remains with its perceiver. To put it into more Western terminology, it would be like saying, each event one experiences teaches a small lesson that will remain forever within the soul of the one who learned it.

The Two Worlds: *Aye* and *Orun*

The Yoruba believe that the world we live in is split into two parallel realms that are closely intertwined. The *aye* is the tangible, visible world that all sentient beings experience everyday; the *orun* is the spiritual invisible realm inhabited by gods, ancestors and spirits. This is often represented and conceptualized as a flat, circular divination tray with a raised, fancifully engraved border. Often, the pictures and images along the circumference of the tray represent mythological events, people or can simply be related to quotidian events and affairs—the main take away is the symbolism of a complex world full of forces that are constantly interacting and competing with one another. Further, at the outset of a divination (the act of seeking knowledge of the future or the unknown via supernatural means) a diviner will inscribe intersecting lines on the flat surface of the divination tray. Such lines are referred to as *orita meta*, literally "the point of intersection between [both] cosmic realms." These lines are always drawn at the beginning of the divination ritual in order to open up spiritual channels of communication before the diviner can reveal the meaning of the lines.

The *Orun*: The World of the Spirits, Gods and Ancestors

Oludumare (a.k.a. *Odumare, Olorun, Eleda* and *Eleemi*) would be the equivalent of God in Christianity. *Oludumare* is thus believed to be the creator of all things in existence. However, there is not a gender attached to this deity and it maintains a strictly *laissez-faire* relationship with respect to both human and divine affairs. More importantly, *Oludumare* is the source of each sentient beings' *ase*, or life force.

The *orisa*, namely the "deified ancestors and/or personified natural forces" fall into two categories. They are either of the *orisa funfun*, the "cool, temperate and symbolically white" or of the *orisa gbigbona*, the "hot, temperamental gods." Those gods belonging to the *orisa funfun* are usually mild mannered, calm, "soothing, reflective" and consist of the following divinities :
Obatala/Orisanla: the divine sculptor
Osoosi/Eyinle: hunter and water lord
Osanyin: lord of leaves and medicines
Oduduwa: first monarch at Ile-Ife, the cradle of the Yoruba civilization
Yemoja, Osun, Yewa and *Oba*: queens of their respective rivers

Many of the *orisa gbigbona* tend to be male, however, not all of them. They themselves include:
Ogun: god of iron
Sango: former king of *Oyo* and lord of thunder
Obaluaye: lord of pestilence
Oya: *Sango's* wife and queen of the whirlwind

The division of the *orisa* has nothing to do with good and evil; rather, just as humans are believed to contain both good and bad attributes, the *orisa* themselves are viewed in this light. Even more interesting, the Yoruba pantheon is not a hierarchy. Therefore *Oludumare*, although creator of all things is not viewed as the King of *orun* in an absolutist sense; instead, the importance attached to any given *orisa* is more a reflection of their popularity in a given region.

All deities contained within the Yoruba pantheon are believed to periodically enter the *aye*, and thus can interact and provide guidance, or interfere maliciously in human affairs. However, two important deities, *Ifa* and *Esu/Elegba*, are essentially the gatekeepers between *orun* and *aye*. *Ifa*, "actually a Yoruba system of divination, is presided over by *Orunmila*, its mythic founder" who also sometimes may be referred to as *Ifa*. *Esu/Elegba* "is the divine messenger and activator." It is a central belief of the Yoruba people that *Ifa* provides them a means by which to understand the forces that influence their lives on a daily basis; this can be achieved in a variety of ways, most notably sacrifice and prayer. A diviner, known as *babalawo*, literally "father of ancient wisdom" will use a variety of methods to communicate with the inhabitants of *orun*, or to identify the "enemies of humankind," namely: "Death, Disease, Infirmity, and Loss." The *babalawo* may also identify other entities for concern: *egbe abiku* literally "spirit children" that kill newborn babies, or *aje* and *oso*, literally "witches" and "wizards" respectively. In contrast to *Ifa*, a being that can be identified, communicated and reasoned with, *Esu/Elegba*, is unpredictable. *Esu* is the keeper of all the sacrifices to *orun* and the enforcer of all ritual processes. If not properly acknowledged and worshipped, a common Yoruba expression warns, "life is the bailing of waters with a sieve."

The ancestors, collectively known as "*oku orun, osi, babanla* and *iyanla*" are the other major group inhabiting *orun*. Although they are no longer living in the realm of the living, they are not viewed as being deceased, as in Christianity. They can still be communicated with and are an important source of guidance within Yoruba culture. This can be achieved in one of two ways: (i) via masked diviners known as the *egungun* or (ii) or by speaking with living relatives who are often believed to be partial reincarnations of departed ancestors. As an example, consider a female child that a diviner realizes is an incarnation of her departed grandmother. She would be named *Yetunde*, literally "Mother-has-returned"—the grandmother is believed to remain in *orun* but part of her, her *emi* literally "spirit" or "breath" will reside within the child.

Aye: The Tangible World

A good definition of *aye* is the world in which all sentient beings reside. However, this misses a key concept, namely that it is take as a given in Yoruba culture that the residents of *orun* regularly interact with the living. Thus, the aye also includes these interactions and at times can even contain, at different points in time, members of *orun*. The Yoruba saying, "*Aye l'oja, orun n'ile*" best capture this idea and it means, "The world is a marketplace we [all] visit, [and] the otherworld is home." Thus, the Yoruba believe that we all exist forever in the *orun* once we arrive there. The Yoruba also believe that human life is unpredictable and fleeting; another common saying, "*Aye l'ajo, orun n'ile*" meaning "The world [life] is a journey, the other world [afterlife] is home." During one's stay in *aye*, the Yoruba believe that one should strive to achieve: "long life, peace, prosperity, progeny, and good reputation." These are best achieved through seeking to obtain: "wisdom, knowledge" and "understanding."

From the standpoint of social organization and hierarchy, the Yoruba are very open, yet they still possess a monarchy and much social stratification. Just as in the *orun* there is no supreme ruler who dictates public policy; rather policy decisions are made between everyone willing to participate. Similar to the United States, there exists a system of checks-and-balances in order to ensure a fairly equal society. The reason that the Yoruba strive for equality stems from their belief system. Recall that each person is believed to possess an *ase*, or life force, given to them by *Oludumare*. Thus, each person is believed to be inherently equal and ranks exist because a person has striven to obtain "wisdom, knowledge" and "understanding" and has risen to their rank via their own merit.

Ogun: A closer look

As previously mentioned, *Ifa*, god of divination and *Esu*, the god who is responsible for carrying offerings unto the Yoruba pantheon inhabiting *orun* as well as protecting traditional rituals are "widely known and worshiped as *Ogun*." To get a sense of how important *Ogun* is in Yoruba culture, it is logical to explore the extent to which he was worshipped, since this is a direct measure of his significance. "Ogun" counts for "14 percent of all *orisa* reported" throughout *Oyo*. He is third only to *Ifa* and *Esu* who account for 19 and 17 percent of *orisa* reported. Further, when one considers the fact that the aforementioned deities are often collectively worshipped as *Ogun* it becomes even clearer that *Ogun* is a significant deity within the Yoruba pantheon.

Even more is revealed about *Ogun* when one analyzes the traditional Yoruba chants about him:
On the days when *Ogun* is angered,
There is always disaster in the world.
The world is full of dead people going to heaven.
The eyelashes are full of water.
Tears stream down the face.
A bludgeoning by *Ogun* causes a man's downfall.
I see and hear, I fear and respect my *orisa*.
I have seen your [bloody] merriment.

Ogun is considered one of the most powerful deities but on a more fundamental level, he represents the duplicity of man. *Ogun* is endowed with many contradictory traits. He is either "fiery or cool," or can represent both "death and healing." Further, he is often begged for mercy or forgiveness:
Ogun, here is your festival dog.
Do us no harm.
Keep us safe from death.
Do not let the young have accidents
* * * * * * *
Let us have peace.

Soyinka was deeply influenced by *Ogun*, "The philosophy that undergirds [Soyinka's] writings is derived as much from the legends of *Ogun*, the Yoruba god of war and creativity, as from the works of Nietzsche, the modern philosopher of antitradition [*sic*] and rebellion."

Ogun's many contradictory personality traits come out as a major theme within the novel, namely the duplicity of man and nature, which is exemplified in the struggle of the native Africans to carry out their ritual, while the British try as they might to stop them. Further, the intervention of the British into matters about which they understand little has unintended consequences; *Olunde*, the eldest of the horseman's sons, commits suicide in order to fulfill his father's obligation in the uncompleted ritual. This is an exact incarnation of *Esu* and *Ogun* within the play; they have literally entered *aye* and influenced the chain of human events, ensuring that the ritual was successfully performed and since *Elesin* was not complicit, they took away his son from him as punishment. This punishment ultimately drove him to commit suicide in shackles at the play's dramatic end.

Themes and Motifs

Duty

Anti-colonialism is considered a theme by some scholars based on aspects of the text, but Soyinka specifically calls the colonial factors "an incident, a catalytic incident merely" in the "Author's Note" prepended to the play.

Human Understanding of Life and

Death

In the play, the underlying theme of understanding shows how all humans struggle to comprehend each other, life and death. First, the theme of understanding is explored through the English colonists and their cultural tension with the native Yoruba people. In the Second Act, the District Officer, Pilkings, and his wife, Jane, first confront the theme of understanding when they dress up for a ball wearing native death costumes. They see no problem with it, but Mr. Pilkings' employee, Amusa, a native policeman, is frightened by them wearing the costumes, believing it to be bad for people to touch this cloth of death. Although this situation could be looked at on the surface as "clash of cultures," a deeper conflict, involving understanding and respect relating to each other and to death, is also present.

Later in the play, Jane, who is still wearing the costume, meets with Elesin's European educated son, Olunde who tells her that he has "discovered that you have no respect for what you do not understand". Jane is angry with his view, but they continue to visit. Olunde is frustrated at her inability to try to understand or at least to respect that someone else might have a different view of death from her own. While this scene seems well suited to a "clash of cultures" interpretation, it can also be seen as an examination of the basic human understanding of death, and the roadblocks humans encounter—both cultural (in Jane's case) and spiritual (in the case of Elesin and the natives). The reader is shown that it is almost impossible for Jane, as a human, to understand and respect these ideas which she has been conditioned against.

At the end of the story, when Pilkings is talking with Elesin in the cell, the theme of understanding is once more brought out. "You don't quite understand it all but you know that tonight is when what ought to be must be brought about," Elesin tells Pilkings. In this sentence, Elesin alludes to both his death ritual and the cultural gap, uniting the threnodic and cultural themes into one of understanding. Finally, Olunde, talking with Pilkings—who he thinks has just come from witnessing Elesin's death—sums up a main aspect of the theme of understanding which relates to both cultural differences and death, saying, "you must know by now there are things you cannot understand—or help".

The play is not completely just a struggle of understanding for the colonists. The larger struggle is inside the minds of Elesin and the Yoruba people as they try to understand death and the transition into death. In the first scene, this is especially apparent as Elesin prepares for death and the Praise-singer spouts a flood of questions aimed at finding answers to the mystery of death. "There is only one world to the spirit of our race," the Praise-singer says. "If that world leaves its course and smashes on boulders of the great void, whose world will give us shelter?" Here he is trying to gain understanding about what would happen if Elesin isn't successful in carrying out his death ritual. He struggles to know what their fate would be. Later, as Elesin is further into his transition into death, the Praise-singer asks him questions about what he is experiencing, hoping to gain an understanding. "Is there now a streak of light at the end of the passage, a light I dare not look upon?" he asks. "Does it reveal whose voices we often heard, whose touches we often felt, whose wisdoms come suddenly into the mind when the wisest have shaken their heads and murmured; It cannot be done?" He continues, "Your eyelids are glazed like a courtesan's, is it that you see the dark groom and master of life?" In these passages, the Praise-singer represents our "human" questions, and he hopes Elesin, in his half-earthly, half-heavenly state, will help him to understand. But Elesin cannot answer him, and all remains a mystery.

Near the end of the story, the theme of understanding again shows through when Elesin is pondering his failure to fulfil the death ritual. He laments his weakness but also his lack of understanding that led to his failure. He realizes that his failure was tied to a misunderstanding, believing that perhaps the intervention of the colonists was the work of the gods. He is frustrated at his weakness and the catastrophe that came to be as a result. Soon after this realization, Iyaloja reinforces the theme of understanding while arguing with Pilkings: "Child," she says, "I have not come to help your understanding. [Points to Elesin] This is the man whose weakened understanding holds us in bondage to you". The play ends with Iyaloja reminding Elesin's new bride to "forget the dead, forget even the living. Turn your mind only to the unborn". Neither an understanding of people nor death has been reached, but considerable examination and contemplation have occurred. As Iyaloja suggests, one can only concentrate on the future and continue trying to understand the world and the world beyond life.

Yoruba Proverbs

Almost every character in *Death and the King's Horseman* at some point uses a traditional Yoruba proverb. Through his vast knowledge of Yoruba proverbs, Soyinka is able to endow his play with a strong Yoruba sentiment.

Characters often employ Yoruba proverbs primarily as a means of bolstering their opinions and persuading others to take their point of view.

The Praise-singer gets annoyed with *Elesin* for his decision to take a new wife and tries to dissuade him:
Because the man approaches a brand-new bride he forgets the long faithful mother of his children.
Ariyawo-ko-iyale
Similarly, *Iyaloja* tries to admonish *Elesin* against his earthly attachments and stay true to the ritual upon which the good of his society depended:
Eating the awusa nut is not so difficult as drinking water afterwards.
Ati je asala [awusa] ko to ati mu omi si i.
Another common way in which Soyinka uses proverbs is with *Elesin. Elesin* himself uses several proverbs in order to convince his peers that he is going to comply with their ritual and thus join the ancestors in *orun*:
The kite makes for wide spaces and the

wind creeps up behind its tail; can the kite say less than thank you, the quicker the better?
Awodi to'o nre Ibara, efufu ta a n'idi pa o ni Ise kuku ya.
The elephant trails no tethering-rope; that king is not yet crowned who will peg an elephant.
Ajanaku kuro ninn 'mo ri nkan firi, bi a ba ri erin ki a ni a ri erin
The river is never so high that the eyes of a fish are covered.
Odu ki ikun bo eja l'oju
The final way in which proverbs appear in the play is when *Iyaloja* and the Praise-singer harass *Elesin* while he is imprisoned for failing to complete his role within the ritual:
What we have have no intention of eating should not be help up to the nose.
Ohun ti a ki i je a ki ifif run imu
We said you were the hunter returning home in triumph, a slain buffalo pressing down on his neck; you said wait, I first must turn up this cricket hole with my toes.
A ki i ru eran erin lori ki a maa f'ese wa ire n'ile
The river which fills up before our eyes does not sweep us away in its flood.
Odo ti a t'oju eni kun ki igbe 'ni lo

Performances

Written in five acts, it is performed without interruption. "The play is seldom performed outside of Africa. Soyinka himself has directed important American productions, in Chicago in 1979 and at Lincoln Center in New York in 1987, but these productions were more admired than loved. Although respected by critics, Soyinka's plays are challenging for Westerners to perform and to understand, and they have not been popular successes."

The play was performed at London's Royal National Theatre beginning in April 2009, directed by Rufus Norris, with choreography by Javier de Frutos and starring Lucian Msamati. It was also performed at the Oregon Shakespeare Festival from February 14 to July 5, 2009.

Reviews

Death and The King's Horseman "forge[s] out of this story a metaphor not just for the whole history of Africa and its collision with colonial Europe but a profound meditation on the nature of man, . . . the relationship of life with death and the power of religion, ritual and spirituality in human existence." It is probably Soyinka's greatest work for the theatre and remains one of his most universal and accessible dramatic statements.

One of the play's interpretive problems is Elesin's attempt to commit suicide. As Soyinka conceals the moment when Elesin is interrupted, we do not know whether the interruption prevented his follow through, whether he could not bring himself to commit the act, or whether he just did not know how to perform it. He himself gives conflicting explanations, at one time telling his bride that his attraction to her made him long to stay in the world a while longer ("...perhaps your warmth and youth brought new insights of this world to me and turned my feet leaden on this side of the abyss"), while a few moments later telling the village matriarch that he thought the white man's intervention "might be the hand of the gods".

Source http://en.wikipedia.org/wiki/Death_and_the_King's_Horseman

Egungun

Egungun is a part of the Yoruba pantheon of divinities. In the indigenous religious system of the West African tribe of that name, the spirit is of central importance. It is the eventual end of all living beings, and as such is regarded as the ancestral "collective".

Function

Amongst the Yoruba, the annual ceremonies in honour of the dead serve as a means of assuring their ancestors a place among the living. They believe the ancestors have the responsibility to compel the living to uphold the ethical standards of the past generations of their clan, town or family. The Egungun is celebrated in festivals, known as **Odun Egungun**, and in family ritual through the masquerade custom.

In family situations, a family elder known either formally or informally as "Alagba" presides over ancestral rites. He may or may not be initiated into the local Egungun society. In matters that deal with whole communities, Egungun priests and initiates who are trained in ancestral communication, ancestral elevation and funerary rites are assigned to invoke and bring out the ancestors. They wear elaborate costumes in masquerade. Through drumming and dance, the Egungun robed performers are believed to become possessed of the spirits of the ancestors, as manifested as a single entity. The Egungun spiritually clean the community; through the dramatic acting and miming of the robed priests, they demonstrate both ethical and amoral behavior that have occurred since their last visit. In this way, they expose the strengths and weaknesses of the community to encourage behavior more befitting of their descendants. When this performance is completed, the performers as Egungun give messages, warnings and blessings to the assembled spectators.

Important Egungun include the Oloolu and Alapansanpa, both of Ibadanland. Elewe of the Ìgbómìnà Yoruba clan, which is common in the towns of Òkè-Ìlá Òràngún, Ìlá Òràngún, and Arandun, is also of particular prominence.

In Brazil, the main cult of the Egungun is found on the island of Itaparica, in the State of Bahia. Houses of worship dedicated to the Egungun also exist in other states.

Source http://en.wikipedia.org/wiki/Egungun

A Egungun masquerade dance garment in the permanent collection of The Children's Museum of Indianapolis

Epa mask

An **Epa mask** is a ceremonial mask worn by the Yoruba people of Nigeria during the Epa masquerade. Carvings representing priests, hunters, farmers, kings, and mothers are usually depicted on the masks. They are used to acknowledge important roles within the community, and to honor those who perform the roles, as well as ancestors who performed those roles in the past.

When not being used during performances, Epa masks are kept in shrines where they are the focus of prayers and offerings from community elders.

Source http://en.wikipedia.org/wiki/Epa_mask

Epa mask, collection of the Horniman Museum

Ibeji

Pair of ibeji, authenticated by the Department of Antiquities of Nigeria

Ibeji (Yoruba: *Ìbejì*) is a term in the Yoruba language meaning "twins".

Overview

The Yoruba are a major African ethnic group; in their culture twins are traditionally very important beings. In the Yoruba language "ibeji" literally means "twins". Carved wooden figures made to house the soul of a dead twin are also called ibeji. These wooden figures, six to ten inches high and carved with the family mask, are often well tended. The Yoruba people believe that this care and tending helps ensure the survival of the other twin. In the Yoruba traditional religion, there is a deity that represents twins called Orisha Ibeji or Orisa Ibeji.

Origins

While the birth rate of monozygotic twins is relatively constant worldwide, about 4 per 1000 births, that rate for dizygotic twins varies widely. The incidence of dizygotic twin births in much of Africa is significantly greater than in the United States, with the highest incidence among the Yoruba peoples of Nigeria, with a frequency of 45 per 1000 births. In fact, the Yoruba town of Igboora boasts of an average of 150 twins for 1000 births and is therefore considered Nigeria's, and the world's, capital of twins.

Practice

A pair of female ere ibeji twin figures (early 20th-century) in the permanent collection of The Children's Museum of Indianapolis

Traditionally, when twins were born, the parents would visit a Babalawo, meaning, "father of mysteries", to find out their wishes. The first of the twins to be born is traditionally named Taiyewo or Tayewo, (which means 'the first to taste the world'); this is often shortened to Taiwo, Taiye, or Taye. Kehinde, "the last to come", is the name of the last-born twin. These are what could be called "celestial" Yoruba names; names due to birth circumstances. The child after the twins is called "Idowu" regardless of the sex, a boy or a girl. "Alaba" is the one after Idowu, either a boy or a girl, which is usually followed by "Oni" and "Ola" or "Idogbe".

It is said that Kehinde sends Taiyewo to check out what life is like on earth and to tell him (or her) whether it is good. Therefore, Taiyewo goes as sent by Kehinde, and becomes the first child to be born. He then communicates to Kehinde spiritually (believed to be from the way he cries) whether life is going to be good or not. The reply determines if Kehinde will be born alive or stillborn. Both return to where they came from if the reply from Taiyewo is not good enough for both of them.

The Yoruba traditionally say that Kehinde is the true elder of the twins despite being the last to be born, because he sent Taiyewo on an errand, a prerogative of one's elders in Yorubaland. Kehinde is therefore referred to as Omokehindegbegbon (which means, "the child that came last becomes the elder"). However, the first-born twin is also sometimes referred to as Taiyelolu or Tayelolu, which is short for Omotaiyelolu and means, "the child that came to taste life excels".

Since in Yoruba tradition, each person is one soul in the long line of ancestral souls, twins are complex, sharing the same soul - but one of the two is thought to have the spiritual half of the soul while the other has the mortal half. Since there is no way to determine which has the mortal soul and which the spiritual soul, if one twin should die, a carving is commissioned to represent the deceased child. Only the sex and the lineal facial scarifications (if the child had any) are specified and are faithfully recreated in the carved figure. Taiyewo is believed to be mostly the quiet, calmer, and introverted of the twins, while Kehinde is mostly believed to be the extroverted one.

Ere ibeji

As stated above, the Yoruba believe that both twins share one soul, so if one twin dies at a young age, the balance of the soul is thrown off or disturbed. The death rate of children is very high in Africa, and on account of this, a ritual is carried out to put the twins' soul back into balance. The Ifá priest chooses a well-established carver to create a small figure that symbolizes the dead child. The carver is free to create a figure of the twin in his own image of what he felt about the twin. If both twins die, then two figures are made. The soul is then spiritually transported into the figures. These figures are called ere ibeji. Ibi means born, eji means two, and ere means sacred image. The figure remains as respected and as powerful as the person it represents. The children's parents must treat the statue as if it were real, so it is bathed, fed, and clothed just as it would be in life. The figure is particularly special to the mother, who keeps the figure close to her bed. She rubs the figure with red wood powder to maintain the look of slickness, and she caresses the figure in a loving manner. Rituals and prayers are performed for the child's birthday and other celebrations or festivals.

The head of the figure is associated with the child's destiny, which measures the success or failure of the child. The size of the head is one-third the size of the body because the head is where the spirit resides. The head must be big in proportion to the rest of the body. The figure is very detailed, but it is only a symbol of the child and is not intended to be a realistic likeness but rather a resemblance of a human. The child is shown as an adult, which is common in African sculpture. The features of the child are more mature, including scarifications on the face, and full-sized breasts on female figures. The surface of the figure is very smooth. The figure is motionless to represent discipline, serenity, and confidence. The figure is sometimes made to hold symbolic items. Shells or beads may invoke certain gods or indicate wealth.

Source http://en.wikipedia.org/wiki/Ibeji

Ifá

Sixteen Principal Odu

Name	1	2	3	4
Ogbe	I	I	I	I
Oyẹku	II	II	II	II
Iwori	II	I	I	II
Odi	I	II	II	I
Irosun	I	I	II	II
Iwọnrin	II	II	I	I
Ọbara	I	II	II	II
Ọkanran	II	II	II	I
Ogunda	I	I	I	II
Ọsa	II	I	I	I
Ika	II	I	II	II
Oturupọn	II	II	I	II
Otura	I	II	I	I
Irẹtẹ	I	I	II	I
Ọsẹ	I	II	I	II
Ofun	II	I	II	I

Sixteen Principal Afa-du

(Yeveh Vodou)

Name	1	2	3	4
Eji-Ogbe	I	I	I	I
Ọyeku-Meji	II	II	II	II
Iwori-Meji	II	I	I	II
Odi-Meji	I	II	II	I
Irosun-Meji	I	II	II	II
Ọwanrin-Meji	II	II	II	I
Ọbara-Meji	I	I	II	II
Ọkanran-Meji	II	II	II	I
Ogunda-Meji	I	I	I	II
Ọsa-Meji	II	I	I	I
Ika-Meji	I	I	II	I
Oturupon-Meji	I	II	I	I
Otua-Meji	II	II	I	II
Irete-Maji	II	I	II	II
Ọse-Meji	I	II	I	II
Ofu meji	II	I	II	I

Ifá refers to the system of divination and the verses of the literary corpus known as the Odú Ifá. Yoruba religion identifies Orunmila as the Grand Priest; as that which revealed Oracle divinity to the world. Such is his association with the Oracle divinity; in some instances, the term "Orunmila" is used interchangeably with Ifá.

Originating in West Africa in the form of a stringent Yoruba philosophy; celebrated in traditional African medicine, Santería (referred to as Lukumi), Candomblé, West African & Diaspora Vodou, and similarly in Orisa'Ifa lineages all over the globe.

Yorùbá canon

In the Yoruba religion, divination gives priests unreserved access to the teachings of Orunmila. Esu, is seen as being in charge of justice and order and the transportation of ebos. Esu is the one said to lend authority (*ase*) to the oracle during provision of direction and or clarification of counsel. Esu is also the one that holds the keys to ones Ire (blessings), thus acts as Oluwinni (ones Creditor), he can grant Ire or remove it read more about this Yoruba concept of Oluwinni here. Ifa divination rites are claimed to provide an avenue of communication to the spiritual realm and the intent of ones destiny.

Togo canon

In Togo, Ifá is known as **Afa**, where the Vodou deities come through and speak. In many of their Egbes, it is *Alaundje* who is honored as the first Bokono to have been taught how to divine the destiny of humans using the holy system of Afa.

International recognition

The Ifa Divination system was added in 2005 by UNESCO to its list of the "Masterpieces of the Oral and Intangible Heritage of Humanity".

Divination

Performing Ifa divination is called Ifa dida or idafa (ounte ale). Ifa dida / Idafa is performed by a Babalawo or Iyalawo or iyanifa (an initiated priest or priestess). *Babalawo* can be translated as "father of the secrets" while "Iyalawo" {mother of secret} or sometimes "Iyanifa" means "mother that has Ifa(i.e. its blessing)". The babalawo or iyanifa provides insights about the current circumstances impacting the life of a person requesting this information and provides any necessary information to aid the individual. Awo is a reference for devotees in Orisa worship. It includes Babalawos, Iyalawo, Iyanifas, Babalorishas, Iyalorishas and even uninitiated devotees. Traditionally, women have not been initiated into Ifa priesthood, according to the teaching which allows them only a single Ikin. In the USA a small sect of worshipers has initiated women into Ifa. These initiations are however only recognized by that group.

Occasions

Ifa divination (also called consultation) is performed for many proposes and a host of occasions, the purposes and occasions is what determines the instrument used in the divination sessions. Divination is often performed for lesser reasons such as "regular check up" to life-changing occasions such as marriage or child birthing etc., divination can also be performed for a group (small / large) or community (the first examples are more likely for a person, couple, parents or family). On occasion when it is performed for the community or society it takes on another significance. Below we will list and discuss major occasions divination is performed and give some feedback and examples of each, in application and practice.

Annual Divination for the New Year - one occasion where a major divination is performed and the ranking Ifa Priest are present to witness and partake. This is called the divination of the new year, which is also sometimes referred to as the First Yam Festival (for ancient annual agricultural cycles). For the current year 2012 / 2013 (the Yoruba year begins early June for a 12 month cycle), is the holy Odu Ifa Ogbe Ogunda (alias Ogbe Iyonu/ OgbeYonu / OgbeYono and Ogbe Suuru etc. each alias has special meaning). The results of such a divination will be discussed and analyzed by the ranking Ifa Priest, shared with the Ooni (the ruling King of Yoruba People), and shared with the extended community. To read more about the governing Odu for 2012 & 2013, click here.

Establishing a new town or settlement, is another reason Ifa is cast to know more about that towns living principals and parameters etc. An example can be found in IrosunMeji.

Mate selection - (or courting) a potential partner, several examples will be posted shortly.

Esentaye (new born baby rites) - Also called Ikosedaye, is another major occasion to consult Ifa for direction and advice

Burial rites

Planning a new business or enterprise etc.

Etiquette

Initiation into Ifa requires rigorous study. A Babalawo must learn and understand each of the 256 chapters (Odu) of Ifa. The minimum of four verses will of necessity include ebos and ooguns (medicine) that are embedded and relevant to each of the verses, plus other issues that complement divination. An accomplished Babalawo must know about ten verses of each of the 256 chapters of Ifa (256 Odu Ifa). Regardless of gender, whoever aspires to practice Ifa must have this qualification. In essence, Ifa practice does not preclude a woman provided such woman acquires the required qualification. Odu — a special Orisa — can only be received by a Babalawo who decides to perform the special initiation that will allow him access to Odu. In essence, initiation into Ifa is the first step towards initiation into Odu. A woman cannot be initiated into Odu. This is because since she already has a womb, she has no need to receive Odu. It can be said to be redundant. Character Traits of an Awo: Orunmila demands humility from his priests and priestesses, therefore, a Babalawo should be an embodiment of patience, good character, honesty, and humility.

On the other hand, in Cuba and parts of Nigeria such as Ode Remo, Ijebuland and Ibadan (and Ile Ife up until at least 1992), the position of the Iyanifa as a divining priestess of Ifa is hotly contested on the grounds that in the Ifa Odus Ogunda Ka, Irete Intelu and Oshe Yekun, no one can become a full Awo Ifa without the presence of Odun, and in the Odu Ifa Irete Ntelu (Irete Ogbe), Odun herself says that she would only marry Orunmila if he promised not to permit women to be in the same room as her. Also, Dr. Ikulomi Djisovi Eason reports that in Ile Ife, widely considered Ifá's capital among traditional Yoruba, did not initiate women as late as 1992. These views appear to be confirmed by books published in Nigeria as far back as the 19th century. For instance, the eminent Yoruba author James Johnson wrote in one of the most detailed early descriptions of Ifa that "Whenever this should be the case, a woman would receive from a Babalawo only one Ikin or Consecrated Palm nut called Eko, which she would carry about her body for her protection, and whenever divination should recommend and prescribe to her sacrifice to Ifa, she would, for the time being, hand over her Eko either to her husband or to her brother, or any other male relative according to prescription, who would include it in his own Ikins for the purpose of the worship and sacrifice in which she would participate." William Bascom, the foremost academic authority on Ifa up until the time of his death, also stated that "only men can become babalawo" and that he never encountered a single female Ifa priest acting as a diviner during any of his extensive field studies in the cities of Ife, Igana, Meko, Oyo, Ilesa, Abeokuta, Osogbo, Sagamu, Ilara, Ondo, Ijebu Ode or Ekiti in Yorubaland in 1937-38, 1950–51, in 1960 and 1965, nor did any of his informants mention such a thing. Sources from Yorubaland going back to the mid-19th century clearly state that only men can become Ifa diviners. The idea that any woman's womb is the equivalent of Odu, the force that created the universe, is not a tenable one to traditionalists. This is the theological equivalent to a man who might want to claim to be a Babalawo without initiation due to the virtue of having male genitalia as does the Orisha Orunmila.

Apetebi is a title given to the wife of a Babalawo. Apetebi is the name Orunmila gave to his wife, whom he cured from leprosy before giving birth to his child. This is from the Sacred Odu Ifa Obara Ogunda.

Iyanifa is the title of an initiated female priestess of IFA, but can mean several other things as well depending on region and tradition.

Process

Special instruments are used to assist in the divination to transcribe Orunmila's wisdom through the diviner. The items used for divination include:

Tray and palm nuts

a group of sixteen Ikin, commonly known as sacred palm nuts, which are used to create ancient binary data
Dust from the Irosun tree (Iyerosun)
a vessel for the seeds (Ajere Ifa)
a divination tray (*Opon Ifa*).
a tapper instrument (*Iroke Ifa*)
a fly whisk (Irukere Ifa)
beaded belts for the *babalawo/iyanifa* to wear (this is not required)
another form of divination is with the Opele, though Ikin is considered superior
Ifa dida, meaning Ifa consultation/divination also sometimes mistakenly referred to as Dafa
Odù (see Odù Ifá below) revelation (one of possible 256 combinations) and the oral recitation - consultation (ese Ifa)
the "prescription" or advice of what is needed at this particular junction of life. It is believed that ebo (ritual) & bibo (appeasement rites) fit into a category referred to as Ọwọn (necessity) of Odù Ifá; Ọwọnrín Méji, this "necessity or void" once filled is what the deities will use in bringing ones prayers into fruition.
Ifa divination process of "prescription" is organized in three segments in a specific order 1) Ifa Dida (divination) 2) Ebo (ritual rites) 3) Oogun (medicine or healing)
The (opon Ifa) or tray and (iroke Ifa) or tapper are used in Ifa divination, a central ritual within Ifa tradition. This tray, adorned with carved images and dusted with powder, serves as the template on which sacred signs (*odu*) related to the personal concerns of a diviner's client are traced as the point of departure for analysis. In contrast to those transitory signs, the more permanent backdrop of the carved motifs on the tapper and tray constitutes an artistic exegesis of the forces that shape human experience and the universal needs fulfilled by such quests for enlightenment.

To initiate the ritual, the *babalawo/iyanifa* places the tray in front of him and taps rhythmically on it with the pointed end of the tapper, invoking the presence of Orunmila, past diviners, and other Orisa.

There are a variety of Ikin (sacred palm nuts) that are available, but only four "eyes" ikin must be used for ifa divination. The Ikin (sacred palm nuts) are grouped in one hand, then the diviner attempts to shift them all to his/her other hand at once, and counts the remaining Ikin left, hopefully to discover that either one or two remain. (Odu, which are the foundation of the binary data, can only be marked with either one or two palm nuts, remaining in the diviner's original hand. As this process goes on, the diviner marks single or double marks in wood powder spread on his divination tray until he or she has created one of the 256 *odu* that are available.

Each of these *odu* is associated with a traditional set of Ese (poetic tutorials), often relating to Yoruba religion, which explain their divinatory meaning. These tutorials represent thousands of years of observation and are filled with predictions, and both mundane and spiritual prescriptions that resolve issues found in that Odu. Within Ifa, Believers find all the knowledge of the world past, present, and future.

After obtaining the Odu that governs a situation or event, the diviner then determines whether the Odu comes with Ire (signifies good outcome; good times; good news; good luck; e.t.c) or Ibi (which could be viewed as obstacles or impediments to success). After this process the diviner now determines appropriate offerings, spiritual disciplines and/or behavioral changes that are Ọwọn - necessary to bring, keep or compel success for the person receiving divinatory counsel.

Odù Ifá

There are sixteen major books in Odu Ifa literary corpus. When combined there are total of 256 Odu (a collection of sixteen, each of which has sixteen alternatives ⇔ 162, or 44) believed to reference all situations, circumstances, actions and consequences in life based on the uncountable ese (poetic tutorials) relative to the 256 Odu coding. These form the basis of traditional Yoruba spiritual knowledge and are the foundation of all Yoruba divination systems.

Where I is an odd count or a "heads" result, and II is an even count or a "tails" result, the sixteen basic patterns and their Yoruba names are set forth in the sidebar (this is only one way of ordering them, this changes depending on area within Nigeria, or the diaspora. An alternative order used in Ibadan, and Cuba is: Ejiogbe, Oyekun meji, Iwori Meji, Idi Meji, Irosun Meji, Oworin Meji, Obara Meji, Okanran Meji, Ogunda Meji, Osa Meji, Ika Meji, Oturupon Meji, Otura Meji, Irete Meji, Oshe Meji, Ofun Meji. Heepa Odu! This is important to note as it changes the outcomes of certain parts of the reading).

The *babalawo* recites a series of poems with proverbs and stories from the Ifa poetry that go with that choice. The final interpretation is made by the person seeking guidance, who decides how the verses that the *babalawo* has recited should be applied to the problem at hand. (This may be one style, however other schools of thought with Ifa have the Diviner interpreting what Ifa says and not simply chanting and leaving it to the client) Though the number of symbols is different, the Chinese I Ching divination system also bears some resemblance to Ifa divination. Like the I Ching, Ifa combines a large body of wisdom literature with a system for selecting the appropriate passages from it. Unlike the I Ching, however, Ifa poetry is not written down but passed down orally from one *babalawo* to another. Today, there are many texts that are designed to help Babalawos to learn and retain the huge corpus of knowledge.

Belief

Believers deem Ifa as being nothing but the "truth"; functioning to the devoted as not only a system of guidance, but one that fuses way of living with the psychological, providing them with a legitimate course of action that is genuine and unequivocal.

Glossary

Babalawo or Awo Ifa. Male Ifa Priest, literally means Father of secrets

Awo Alatese. This group of Awo have their own specialization within Ifa, mastering the aspects of Ifa preparations

Bokono/Bokonon. (male/female) Priest of Afa/Vodoun

Obomila.(male) priest of Iha/Ifain Benin

Ohen.(male or female)Diviner and Priest

Amengansie. Female oracle priest of Afa/Vodoun (matrilineally inherited).

Akapo. Contrary to common diasporan belief, this is NOT another name for a Babalawo. Rather, it refers to a Babalawo's apprentice who carries the bag (apo in yoruba) containing the Babalawo's divining instruments and related materials. (contradicting view, Apako, does actually refer to babalawos, not just an apprentice, as all babalawos and Orunmila himself, carry their own Ifa in a specially designed bag).

Iyanifa. Female Ifa Priest, can also be a title within an Ifa community or temple, thus Iya ni Ifa, mother who has the knowledge of Ifa, she may also know how to recite Ifa even as a child video seen here. There is some controversy even in Nigeria, not all areas accept Iyanifa. There are several YouTube videos of interviews of chief priests in Ode Remo.

Dida. Divination; using any various Yoruba divination items

Dida Obi. Divination with kola nuts of four or more pieces.

Ifa dida. Divination (dida) of Ifa, using any Ifa divination items (Opele or Ikin etc.)

Dida Owo. Divination with cowrie shells (combination of 4,6,8 but commonly 16).

Ifa Dida. (meaning Ifa Divination), casting of Ifa on Opon Ifa

Ohunte Ale. Inscribing or marking Odu on the Opon Ifa

Opon Ifa. Divining tray of Ifa, used by a Babalawo

Oròrò Ifá - Narration or declaration; making a verbal authoritative declaration during the divination analysis or during the advisement following divination or prayer while performing appeasement. (read more on Oròrò Ifá here)

Ifa Rere. Moral Character - of Ifa ethics

Ifa Pele. Gentle Character - of Ifa ethics

Orunmila. Prophet that developed and spread the Ifa divination system. Orunmila is second only to Olodumare/Olorun (God, or Supreme Being), and is without earthly lineage. He embodies the principles of Ifa.

Orisha. Primordial energies (Ìṣẹ̀ṣe) from which all living things emanate; The deities that represent various manifestations of God, Olodumare.

Iya Nla. Ìyá àgbà, the Womb of Creation, Womb of existence, the fearful power, the Mother of the closed calabash, the Mother of the Gourd, who teaches humankind through Awon Iya Wa how to acquire the cosmic knowledge to understand life, balance and the harmony in their life.

Irunmole. Primordial deities (Ìṣẹ̀ṣe), first sent to earth to make the world habitable for humankind, also the full spectrum of deities (Orisha) created by Olodumare the Creator for worship and veneration numbering 400+1 as an infinite number of nature's manifestation and recreation, also differs from Orisha yet some Irunmole are Orisha.

Ìṣẹ̀ṣe. The name Ìṣẹ̀ṣe can be used to describe several things within the Yoruba tradition, i) Ìṣẹ̀ṣe is considered ones Progenitors, ii) all the Primordial Beings of Creation are also Ìṣẹ̀ṣe, iii) the collective of all the Orisa/Irunmole are Ìṣẹ̀ṣe, iv) also Ìṣẹ̀ṣe is another term used to encapsulate this tradition of Ifa/Orisa as a whole.... Ìṣẹ̀ṣe also in this regard means Traditionalism (read more on Ìṣẹ̀ṣe here)

Ifa dida / Dafa. Dida is to perform divination and dafa means act of casting Ikin Ifa (sacred holy palm kernel) for divination purpose and divine direction in life

Apetebii. is the wife of a Babalawo, she is one of the few titled positions within the Yoruba tradition and holds an important position within the tradition and culture, she will assist her husband in the worship and appeasement of his Ifa, and help to teach children the fundaments of worshipping Ifa as a philosophy. This is not simply a title, but has accompanying initiations that must be performed to hold this title. Can also be referred to as Iyanifa interchangeably.

Ayafa. this wife is often "married" to the Ifa of a Babalawo and can also be married to another man, or even a female child before marriage age or the girl child of a Babalawo who by "marrying" to Ifa, this is a symbolic ceremony and will convey certain blessing and protection to the female.

Itefa, Itelodu, Elegan are different degrees of the initiation process. It is the ritual of performing one's initiation or rite of passage, to determine one's purpose or destiny. It is important to note that performing *Itefa* alone does not make one a Babalawo or Iyanifa; Itefa is one of many steps of apprenticeship to become a Babalawo (a diviner/healer/counsellor). Itefa is the initiation into Ifa generally. *Itelodu*, which is the complete and most comprehensive, is the Ifa initiation which has the presence of the mysteries of Odu and also involves the process of stepping of "Oke Ipori" at a specially-prepared space with Opa Osun called "Ojuore", which represents and re-enacts the boundary between heaven and earth – the location where each person chooses "Ipin" to fine-tune, as a way of being aligned while *elegan* (not done everywhere in Nigeria) is a type of Itefa without the mysteries of Odu and Oju Ore.

Ifá. Is the word of Olodumare encompassing all knowledge of things past, present and future. It is sometimes used interchangeably as the name for the orisha deity Orunmila. Orunmila is the orisha of wisdom and knowledge, who created the system and method for accessing the knowledge of Ifa; and so during the ritual of divination a "client" is said to "consult Ifà". ***D'afa** or more appropriately *Ifa dida*, is the name of the divination ritual itself where one accesses specific verses in the Odu Ifá (the Yoruba sacred texts) given to the priest through arrangements of the sacred palm nuts cast in divination.

Igbadun Ifá. Igbadun Ifa & Igbadun Olodumare, are principals within Ifa thought, the importance of showing Gratitude (also sometimes called Itenilorun - Gratefulness). Within each structured ese (stanza) of Ifa, the matter of Igbadun is mentioned. First from client to Diviner, Diviner to Orunmila, Orunmila to Olodumare etc. (more on Igbadun/Itenilorun here)

Iwa (character) is one of or perhaps the most important human endeavor taught within Ifa literary corpus and every Ifa stanza (or verse) has one portion dedicated to the issue of teaching the Iwa (character or behaviour) that Ifa supports. This Iwa, which Ifa teaches transcends religious doctrine, is central to every human being, and imparts communal, social and civic responsibility that the Creator (Olodumare) supports. Central to this, is the theme of righteousness and practicing good moral behaviour, not seeking for it in the community but becoming an ambassador of Iwa.

Ifá invest with me,
As Éjìwòrì invested interest in his protégée,
Ifá smile upon me,.

Names

Ifa priests, devotees, celebrants and believers sometimes inherit names related to the divinity; typically, but not necessarily, beginning with the term 'Ifa', like Ifadairo, Ifabiyi, Ifadare, Ifabunmi, etc. The first "I" in these names may be omitted to form Fadairo, Fabiyi, Fadare, Fabunmi, Falola, etc. The prefix "Awo" is also used in names ascribing Ifa or the fellowship - Awolalu, Awodele, Awolowo, Awosika, etc. Same applies to Odu, with Odufora, Odutola, Odugbemi etc.

Audio & Video

EkoFa Podcast also an iTunes podcast
Babalawo in Nigeria performing traditional Ibofa-appeasement rites video
Entertainment music of Ifa
Performing Iwefa - cleansing rites video
Ìgbéyàwó-Traditional Ifá/Yoruba wedding video

Resources

Awo Falokun Fatunmbi *Dafa: Ifa Divination*
Awo Falokun Fatunmbi *Awo: Ifa & the Theology of Orisha Divination*
Awo Falokun Fatunmbi *Ibase Orisa*
Awoyinfa Ifaoju writing on "Ifa Speaks" published articles on Ifa ideology, philosophy & cosmology
Chief FAMA *Fundamentals of the Yoruba Religion (Orisa Worship)* ISBN 0-9714949-0-8
Chief FAMA *Practitioners' Handbook for the Ifa Professional* ISBN 0-9714949-3-2
Chief FAMA *Fundamentos de la Religion Yoruba (Adorando Orisa)* ISBN 0-9714949-6-7
Chief FAMA *Sixteen Mythological Stories of Ifa (Itan Ifa Merindinlogun)* ISBN 0-9644247-2-X
Chief FAMA *FAMA'S EDE AWO (Orisa Yoruba Dictionary)* ISBN 0-9644247-8-9
Chief FAMA *The Rituals (novela)* ISBN 0-9644247-7-0
Awo Fasina Falade *Ifa: The Key to Its Understanding* ISBN 0-9663132-3-2
Chief Adedoja Aluko *The Sixteen (16) Major Odu Ifa from Ile-Ife* ISBN 978-37376-6-X
Chief Hounon-Amengansie, Mama Zogbé (Vivian Hunter Hindrew) *Mami Wata: Africa's Ancient God/dess Unveiled Vol. I* ISBN 09716244542
Chief S. Solagbade Popoola library, INC *Ifa Dida: Vol 1* (EjiOgbe - Orangun Meji), ISBN 978-0-9810013-1-9
Chief S. Solagbade Popoola library, INC *Ifa Dida: Vol 2* (Ogbe Oyeku - Ogbe Ofun), ISBN 978-1-926538-12-9
Chief S. Solagbade Popoola & Fakunle Oyesanya *Ikunle Abiyamo - The ASE of Motherhood* ISBN 978-09810013-0-2
C. Osamaro Ibie *Ifism the Complete Works of Orunmila* ISBN 1-890157-05-8
Charles Spencer King *Nature's Ancient Religion: Orisha Worship & IFA* ISBN 1-4404-1733-4
Charles Spencer King *IFA Y Los Orishas: La Religion Antigua De LA Naturaleza* ISBN 1-4610-2898-1
William R. Bascom: *Ifa Divination: Communication Between Gods and Men in West Africa* ISBN 0-253-20638-3
William R. Bascom: *Sixteen Cowries: Yoruba Divination from Africa to the New World* ISBN 0-253-20847-5
Iyanifa Ileana S. Alcamo "The Challenge growing within the Orisa Community" ISBN 1-890157-31-7
Rosenthal, J. *'Possession Ecstasy & Law in Ewe Voodoo"* ISBN 0-8139-1805-7
Maupoil, Bernard. *"La Geomancie L'ancienne Côte des Esclaves*
Alapini, Julien. *Les noix sacrées. Etude complète de Fa-Ahidégoun génie de la sagesse et de la divination au Dahomey*
Iyalaja Ileana Alcamo (2007). *The Source Iya Nla Primordial Yoruba Mother*, Athelia Henrietta Press, Inc. ISBN 1-890157-41-4
Dr. Ron Eglash (1997) American Anthropologist *Recursion in ethnomathematics*, Chaos Theory in West African divination.
Dr. Reginald O. Crosley (2000) *The Voudou Quantum Leap* ISBN 1-56718-173-2
Fakayode Fayemi Fatunde (2004) "Osun, The Manly Woman". New York Athelia Henrietta Press ISBN 1-890157-36-8
Fakayode Fayemi Fatunde (2011) "Iwure: Efficacious Prayer to Olodumare, The Supreme Force". Ibadan: Ejiodi Home of Tradition ISBN 978-978-915-402-9
Fakayode Fagbemijo Amosun (2011) "All Days Are Sacred". Oyeku Ofun Temple
Source http://en.wikipedia.org/wiki/Ifá

Itutu

Itutu, which literally translates as "cool" from the Yoruba language, has been used by the Yoruba and more recently by Africanist art historians to describe the aesthetic that characterizes much Yoruba and some African-American art. An "Itutu" aesthetic includes the appearance of a calm, collected face that is found in much Yoruba sculpture. It has been suggested by Robert Farris Thompson of Yale University that Itutu is the origin of the American idea of the "cool". His 1973 article "An Aesthetic of the Cool" traces the idea of "Itutu" from the Yoruba to several other African civilizations and finally to the Americas, where the descendents of Africans perpetuated the importance of being "cool".

Source http://en.wikipedia.org/wiki/Itutu

Obaala

Obaala (or in Yoruba orthography **Ọbaálá**) is a senior title in the royal council of many kingdoms of the northeastern Yoruba - the Igbomina, Ijẹṣa and Ekiti sub-ethnics.

Ọbaálá literally means "mighty king" or "senior king" and is almost always next in rank to the high king or paramount king of the areas where the title is used. The Ọbaálá is often designated as the automatic regent on the demise of any reigning king or paramount king.

The most famous Ọbaálá in recent Yoruba history is easily Ogedengbe, the Ijẹṣa war commander who co-led the "Ekiti Parapọ", a clan confederation which stood to oppose the imperialism of 19th century Ibadan.

Navigation menu

Source http://en.wikipedia.org/wiki/Obaala

Ọba kò so

Ọba kò so (*The King Did Not Hang*) is a play by Duro Ladipo depicting the mystical and ambivalent personality known as Shango of Yoruba mythology.

Background

Shango is the protagonist of the play, according to some historians, as the king of Oyo, he was a feared figure both by his subjects and across the Niger by the Borgu and Nupe empires. He was known for his warring and tyrannical ways and as a symbol later deified in history and worshiped by some. His era was one of turbulence and also of intrigue. Duro Ladipo, was however influenced by the writings of Samuel Johnson, a Yoruba historian who used a lot of old Oyo sources for his book on the Yoruba's. Duro's play created the image of Sango as a tragic hero.

Plot

The play tries to revisit history by portraying a stout and space consuming Sango, as a leader mindful of the wishes of the people; in his desire to please them, he set two of his most powerful chiefs against each other. The chiefs, Gbonka and Timi had grown too powerful and were becoming a nuisance to the kingdom. However, the plot ended up dividing his cabinet and many of his advisers, friends and a wife, Oya left him.

Shango's friend Mogba, rather than joining the traitors, desired to redeem the battered image of the king. Mogba invoked incantations causing thunder and lightning to damage the homes of Sango's enemies.

Source http://en.wikipedia.org/wiki/Ọba_kò_so

Oduduwa

Oduduwa, Olofin Adimula, oba and founder of the Yoruba people, phonetically written by his people as **Odùduwà** and sometimes contracted as *Odudua* or *Oòdua*, is generally held among the Yoruba to be the ancestor of the crowned Yoruba kings.

Emperor Odùduwà

Odùduwà Atewonron "Jingbinni bi Ate'kun"

Children Olowu
Alaketu
Omo N'Oba
Òràngún
Onisabe
Olupopo
Alaafin

About Oduduwa

Etymology

Oòdua first appears as one of the divinities of the Yoruba theogony; The narrative indicates that *Oduduwa* denotes "the essence of behaviour" (Odu-ti-o-da-Iwa) or "the reservoir of culture or manners"(Odu-ti-o-du-iwa).

Narrative

Oral history of the Oyo-Yoruba recounts the coming of the Oba Oduduwa from the east, sometimes understood by some sources as the "vicinity" of Mecca, but more likely signifying the region of Ekiti and Okun sub-communities in northeastern Yorubaland/central Nigeria. Ekiti is near the confluence of the Niger and Benue rivers, and is where the Yoruba language is presumed to have separated from related ethno-linguistic groupings like Igala, Igbo, and Edo.

When Oduduwa arrived ancient Ife, he and his group are believed to have conquered the component communities and to have evolved the palace structure with its effective centralized power and dynasty. Going by the tribal records, he is commonly referred to as the first Ooni of Ife and progenitor of the Yoruba people.

Some oral traditions claim that Oduduwa was Olodumare's favourite orisha, and as such was sent from heaven to create the earth.

Oduduwa and His role in Creation

There is much controversy concerning him and his place in the Yoruba pantheon, and consensus on the subject is as elusive as it is with any other "creation myth". However, the Ife are known for telling the following story:

A certain number of divinities were to accomplish the task of helping earth develop its crust. On one of these visits Obatala, the King of White Clothes, took to the stage equipped with a mollusk that held in its shell some form of soil; two winged beasts and some cloth like material. Having made palm wine from the palm trees he caused to grow after shaping the planet, he began to drink ; soon falling into a drunken stupor, he was unable to accomplish the task he was originally given. Olodumare then sent Oduduwa to save what was left of the mission. When Oduduwa found the Obatala in a "tipsy" state, he simply took over and completed the tasks. The place which he leaped onto from the heavens and which he redeemed from the water to become land was named Ile-Ife and is now considered the sacred and spiritual heart of Yorubaland. Due to this experience, Obatala is said to have subsequently made it a taboo for any of his devotees to drink palm wine. Forgiven by Olodumare, he was later given the responsibility of molding the physical bodies of human beings; the making of land in this story is said to be a symbolic reference to the founding of the Yoruba kingdoms, and this is why Oduduwa is credited with the achievement.

Embodiment of the Royal Dynasty

Oduduwa is considered as the first of the contemporary dynasty of kings of Ife, a figure who sent his sons and daughters out with crowns to rule over all of the other Yoruba kingdoms, which is why all royal Yoruba lineages claim ambilineal descent from its line of kings and, through it, from Oduduwa. This is also why the Ooni of Ife is regarded as first among equals (popularly rendered in the Latin phrase *primus inter pares*) when amongst his fellow Yoruba monarchs.

Later years

Upon the ending of Oduduwa's time on Earth, there was a dispersal of his children from Ife to the outposts that they had previously founded inorder for them to establish effective control over these places. Each is said to have made his or her mark in the subsequent urbanization and consolidation of the Yoruba confederacy of kingdoms, with each child or grandchild fashioning his or her state after Ile-Ife.

Oduduwa and the line of Olowu

A princess marries a priest and later gives birth to the future crowned king of Owu

Oduduwa and the line of Alaketu

A princess gives birth to the future crowned king of Ketu.

Oduduwa and the line of Omo N'Oba

A prince is crowned king of Benin.

Oduduwa and the line of Òràngún

A prince is crowned king of Ila.

Oduduwa and the line of Onisabe

A prince is crowned king of Sabe.

Oduduwa and the line of Olupopo

A prince is crowned king of Popo.

Oduduwa and the line of Alaafin

A prince is crowned king of Oyo.

Oranmiyan

Oranmiyan was the grandson and the most adventurous of the members of

Oduduwa's household; taking the title of Alafin, he succeeded in raising a very strong army and expanding his kingdom to an empire. Regarded as being founder of the Oyo Kingdom, some accounts state he was also the third ruler of Ife.

Moremi

After the dispersal of the family of kings and queens, the aborigines became ungovernable, and constituted themselves into a serious threat to the survival of Ife. Thought to be survivors of the old occupants of the land that had been before the arrival of Oduduwa, these people turned themselves into marauders. They would come to town in costumes made of raffia with terrible and fearsome appearances, and burn down houses and loot the markets. It is at this point that Moremi Ajasoro, a princess of the Ooduan dynasty by marriage, is said to have come onto the scene; she subsequently played a significant role in restoring normalcy back to the situation through a now fabled spying mission.

Alternative views

An Islamic Scholar

Among the critics of Yoruba traditions about Oduduwa is the London-based Yoruba Muslim scholar, Sheikh Dr. Abu-Abdullah Adelabu, a PhD graduate from Damascus whose followers run several publications. In an interview with a Nigerian media house Sheikh Adelabu, the founder and spiritual leader of Awqaf Africa Society in London, dismissed the common myth that all Yorubas are descendants of Oduduwa as a false representation by Orisha worshippers to gain an unjust advantage over the spread of Islam and the recruitment of Christianity". The Muslim scholar advised his followers at his Awqaf Africa College London against using phrases such as Omo Oduduwa i.e. Children of Oduduwa and Ile-Oduduwa i.e Land of Oduduwa. He argued that the story that all the Yorubas are children of Odua was based only on word of mouth, and that it does not conform with the science and the reality of logic conducted on objective principles which usually consists of systematized experimentation with phenomena, especially when examining materials and functions of the physical and spiritual worlds of the African people."

Source http://en.wikipedia.org/wiki/Oduduwa

Oríkì

Oríkì, or praise poetry, is a cultural phenomenon among the Yòrùbá-speaking people of West Africa.

Oríkì Characteristics

Oríkì varies in length depending on whether it's the name given to a child to describe the future portents of his or her life or a recital of the accomplishments of a person's clan. It is invoked when praising a child for bringing pride to the parents or when attempting to evoke virtuous character traits of bravery, fortitude and perseverance that are believed to be innate in a person due to his or her pedigree.

It is not always clear what was preeminent in the mind of the person who named a child with the shorter praise names e.g. traditionally a boy born with the umbilical cord around his neck is called Òjó (there are exceptions; the Ijebu sub-culture names a boy or girl Àìná), yet the name Òjó has praise poetry that does not even mention this occurrence but implies that the child would be the darling of ladies and might be a little impatient.

Oríkì and surnames

Usually a family derives its last name from a strong, accomplished patriarch or matriarch, and it is not uncommon to find this person's accomplishments recited in the longer version of the oríkì of all of his or her progeny. An excerpt from praise poetry for the name Òjó would be:

" Òjó ò sí nlé, omo adìe d'àgbà "

t'ó bá wà ńlé, á ti pà Ìyà è je....

Examples of Oríkì

Examples of oríkì middle names and their meanings (m and f denote the gender thereof):

Àjoké - meant to be taken care of by all. - f
Àlàké - to take care of her as a result of victory over circumstance. - f
Ànìké - own's property to be taken care of. - f
Àshàké - selected to be spoiled (with good things) - f
Àbèní - begged for (from God or, more traditionally, the gods) - f
Àríké - meant to be spoiled on sight - f
Àdùké - people will fight over the privilege to spoil her - f
Àbèbí - begged for to be birthed (probably a difficult birth) - f
Àdìó - not sure what this means - m
Àjàní - fought to have this child - m
Àkànní - met only once to have this child - m
Àjàgbé - fought to carry this child - m
Àlàò - not sure what this means - m
Àkàndé Àgàn - favourite of the prince - m
Akanni - first male child - m
Source http://en.wikipedia.org/wiki/Oríkì

Orisha

An **Orisha** (also spelled **Orisa** or **Orixa**) is a spirit or deity that reflects one of the manifestations of *Olodumare* (God) in the Yoruba spiritual or religious system. (Olodumare is also known by various other names including **Olorun**, **Eledumare**, **Eleda** and **Olofin-Orun**). This religion has found its way throughout the world and is now expressed in practices as varied as Candomblé, Lucumí/Santería, Shango in Trinidad, Anago and Oyotunji, as well as in some aspects of Umbanda, Winti, Obeah, Vodun and a host of others. These varieties or spiritual lineages as they are called are practiced throughout areas of Nigeria, the Republic of Benin, Togo, Brazil, Cuba, Dominican Republic, Guyana, Haiti, Jamaica, Puerto Rico, Suriname, Trinidad and Tobago, the United States, Uruguay, Argentina and Venezuela among others. As interest in African indigenous religions (spiritual systems) grows, Orisha communities and lineages can be found in parts of Europe and Asia as well. While estimates may vary, some scholars believe that there could be more than 100 million adherents of this spiritual tradition worldwide.

Beliefs

The Yoruba belief in Orisha is meant to consolidate not contradict the terms of Olódùmarè. Adherents of the religion appeal to specific manifestations of Olódùmarè in the form of those whose fame will last for all time. Ancestors and culture-heroes held in reverence can also be enlisted for help with day-to-day problems. Some believers will also consult a geomantic divination specialist, known as a babalawo (Ifa Priest) or Iyanifa (Ifa's lady), to mediate in their problems. Ifa divination, an important part of Yoruba life, is the process through which an adept (or even a lay person skilled in oracular affairs) attempts to determine the wishes of God and His Servants. The cultural and scientific education arm of the United Nations, declared Ifa a Masterpiece of the Oral and Intangible Heritage of Humanity in 2005.

Oduduwa

Oduduwa is considered as the first of the contemporary dynasty of kings of Ife. Cosmicists believe Oduduwa descended from the heavens and brought with him much of what is now their belief system. Migrationists believe Oduduwa was a local emissary from an all too earthly place, said to recount the coming of Oduduwa from the east, sometimes understood by some sources as the "vicinity" of Mecca, but more likely signifying the region of Ekiti and Okun sub-communities in northeastern Yorubaland/central Nigeria.

Ache

Whatever the case may be, all of the Yoruba traditionally believe that daily life depends on proper alignment and knowledge of one's *Ori*. Ori literally means the head, but in spiritual matters it is taken to mean an inner portion of the soul that determines personal destiny and success. *Ase*, which is also spelled "Axe," "Axé," "Ashe," or "Ache," is the life-force that runs though all things, living and inanimate. Ashe is the power to make things happen. It is an affirmation which is used in greetings and prayers, as well as a concept about spiritual growth. Orisha devotees strive to obtain *Ashe* through *Iwa-Pele* or gentle and good character, and in turn they experience alignment with the Ori, or what others might call inner peace or satisfaction with life. Ache is divine energy that comes from Olodumare, the Creator and is manifested through Olorun, who rules the heavens and is associated with the sun. Without the sun, no life could exist, just as life cannot exist without some degree of aché. For practitioners of the Yoruba/Lucumi religion, aché represents a link to the eternal presence of God, the Orishas, and the ancestors.

Pantheon

The Yoruba theogony enjoys a Pantheon of Orishas. this includes: Aganju, Babalu Aye, Erinle, Eshu/Elegba, Yemaya, Nana Buluku, Obà, Obatala, Oxossi/Ochosi/Osoosi, Oshumare, Ogun/Ogoun/Ogunda, Oko, Olofi, Olokun, Olorun, Orunmila, Oshun, Osun, Oya, Ozain, and Shango, among countless others. In the Lucumi tradition, Osun and Oshun are different Orishas. Oshun is the beautiful and benevolent Orisha of love, life, marriage, sex and money while Osun is the protector of the Ori, or our heads and inner Orisha. The Yoruba also venerate their ancestral spirits through Egungun masquerades, Orò, Irumole, Gelede and Ibeji, the orisha of Twins (which is no wonder since the Yoruba are officially known to have the world's highest rate of twin births of any group). In fact, the world capital of twins is the Yoruba town of Igboora, with an average of 150 twins per 1 000 birth.

Partial list of Orishas

Olokun - guardian of the deep ocean, the abyss, and signifies unfathomable wisdom,

Obatala (Obatalá, Oxalá, Orixalá, Orisainlá) - arch-divinity, father of humankind, divinity of light, spiritual purity, and moral uprightness

Orunmila (Orunla, Ifá) - divinity of wisdom, divination, destiny, and foresight

Eshu (Eleggua, Exú, Esu, Elegba, Legbara, Papa Legba) - Eshu is the messenger between the human and divine worlds, Undergod of duality, crossroads and beginnings, and also a phallic and fertility Undergod (an Embodiment of Life) and the deliverer of souls to the underworld (an Embodiment of Death). Eshu is recognized as a trickster and is childlike, while Eleggua is Eshu under the influence of Obatala.

Ochumare (Oshumare, Oxumare) - rainbow deity, divinity of movement and activity, guardian of children and associated with the umbilical cord

Nana Buluku as Yemaja, the female thought of the male creator Ashe and the effective cause of all further creation. Sometimes considered to be the same as the Fon Mawu-Lisa who is, however, most usually depicted as her child or children.

Iemanja (Yemaja, Imanja, Yemayá, Jemanja, Yemalla, Yemana, Yemanja, Yemaya, Yemayah, Yemoja, Ymoja, Nanã, La Sirène, LaSiren, Mami Wata) - divine mother, divinity of the sea and loving mother of mankind, daughter of Obatala and wife of Aganju.

Aganju (Aganyu, Agayu) - Father of Shango, he is also said to be Shango's brother in other stories. Aganju is said to be the orisha of volcanoes, mountains, and the desert.

Shango (Shangó, Xango, Changó,

Chango, Nago Shango) - warrior deity ; divinity of thunder, fire, sky father, represents male power and sexuality

Oba (Obba) - Shango's jealous wife, divinity of marriage and domesticity, daughter of Iemanja

Oya (Oyá, Oiá, Iansã, Yansá, Iansan, Yansan) - warrior deity; divinity of the wind, sudden change, hurricanes, and underworld gates, a powerful sorceress and primary lover of Shango

Ogoun (Ogun, Ogúm, Ogou) - warrior deity; divinity of iron, war, labour, sacrifice, politics, and technology (e.g. railroads)

Oshun Oshún, Qşun, Oxum, Ochun, Osun, Oschun) - divinity of rivers, love, feminine beauty, fertility, and art, also one of Shango's lovers and beloved of Ogoun

Ibeji - the sacred twins, represent youth and vitality

Ochosi (Oxósse, Ocshosi, Osoosi, Oxossi) - hunter and the scout of the orishas, deity of the accused and those seeking justice or searching for something

Ozain (Osain, Osanyin) - Orisha of the forest, he owns the Omiero, a holy liquid consisting of many herbs, the liquid through which all saints and ceremonies have to proceed. Ozain is the keeper and guardian of the herbs, and is a natural healer. He sometimes appears as a beautiful wood sprite when in female form.

Babalu Aye (Omolu, Soponna, Shonponno, Obaluaye, Sakpata, Shakpana) - divinity of disease and illness (particularly smallpox, leprosy, and now AIDS), also orisha of healing and the earth, son of Iemanja

Erinle (Inle) - orisha of medicine, healing, and comfort, physician to the gods

Oko (Okko) - orisha of agriculture and the harvest

Ori (Yoruba) - Ruler of the head

Eshu/Eleggua

Iansan/Iansã, Orixá of wind, change
Nanã, The oldest Orixá in Candomblé
Pair of Ibeji
Babalu Aye/Omolú
Iansan/Iansã
Source http://en.wikipedia.org/wiki/Orisha

Ori (Yoruba)

Ori is a metaphysical concept important to Yoruba spirituality and way of life.

Ori, literally meaning "head," refers to one's spiritual intuition and destiny. It is the reflective spark of human consciousness embedded into the human essence, and therefore is often personified as an Orisha in its own right . In Yoruba tradition, it is believed that human beings are able to heal themselves both spiritually and physically by working with the Orishas to achieve a balanced character, or *iwa-pele*. When one has a balanced character, one obtains an alignment with one's Ori or *divine self*.

Alignment with one's Ori brings, to the person who obtains it, inner peace and satistaction with life. To come to know the Ori is, essentially, to come to know oneself. The primacy of individual identity is best captured in a Yoruba proverb: "Ori la ba bo, a ba f'orisa sile". When translated, this becomes *It is the inner self we ought to venerate, and let divinity be.*

Further reading

Ori Mi Gbe Mi: Ori, Support Me by Fagbemijo Amosun Fakayode
Charles Spencer King.,"Nature's Ancient Religion" ISBN 978-1-4404-1733-7
Charles Spencer King, "IFA Y Los Orishas: La Religion Antigua De LA Naturaleza" ISBN 1-4610-2898-1
Source http://en.wikipedia.org/wiki/Ori_(Yoruba)

The Lion and the Jewel

The Lion and the Jewel is a play by Wole Soyinka first performed in 1959. It chronicles how Baroka, the lion, fights with the modern Lakunle over the right to marry Sidi, the titular Jewel. Lakunle is portrayed as the civilized antithesis of Baroka and unilaterally attempts to modernize his community and change its social conventions for no reason other than the fact that he can. The transcript of the play was first published in 1962 by Oxford University Press.

Characters

Main characters

Baroka - The Balè or reigning chieftain of Ilujinle, a Yoruba village in the realm of the Ibadan clan. A crafty individual, he is the Lion referred to in the title. At sixty-two years of age, he has already sired sixty-three children.

Lakunle - The progressive and absurdly arrogant Westernised teacher. He is in his twenties.

Sidi - A beautiful, yet somewhat egotistical village girl who is wooed by both Baroka and Lakunle. She is the Jewel in the title.

Sadiku - The sly chieftess of the Balè's harem.

Ailatu - Baroka's favourite, but not so towards the end of the drama due to an altercation over Baroka's choice to take a new wife.

Supporting characters

Village girls, a wrestler, a surveyor, schoolboys, his assorted consorts and various musicians, dancers, mummers, prisoners, traders and so on.

Plot

The play takes place over the span of a day (Sunday). It is divided into three parts; morning, noon, and night.

Morning

A schoolteacher is teaching a class the times table when Sidi walks past carrying a pail of water on her head. The teacher peers out of the window and disappears. Two 11-year-old schoolboys start ogling her, so he hits them on the head and leaves to confront her. At this point, we find out that the schoolteacher is Lakunle. He is described as wearing a threadbare and rumpled clean English suit that is a little too small for him. He wears a tie that disappears beneath his waistcoat. His trousers are ridiculously oversized, and his shoes are blanco-white. He comes out and insists on taking the pail from Sidi. She refuses, saying that she would look silly. Lakunle retorts, saying that he told her not to carry loads on her head or her neck may be shortened. He also tells her not to expose so much of her cleavage with the cloth she wears around her breasts. Sidi says that it is too inconvenient for her to do so. She scolds him, saying that the village thinks him stupid, but Lakunle says that he is not so easily cowed by taunts. Lakunle also insults her, saying that her brain is smaller than his. He claims that his books say so. Sidi is angry.

When they are done arguing, Sidi wants to leave, but Lakunle tells her of his love for her. Sidi says that she does not care for his love. Eventually, we find out that Sidi does not want to marry him because Lakunle refuses to pay her bride-price as he thinks it a uncivilised, outrageous custom. Sidi tells him that if she did so, people will jeer at her, saying that she is not a virgin. Lakunle further professes how he wants to marry her and treat her "just like the Lagos couples I have seen". Sidi does not care. She also says that she finds the Western custom of kissing repulsive. She tells him that not paying her bride price is mean and miserly.

Enter the village girls. They decide to play "the dance of the Lost Traveller". They tease the traveller in the play, calling his motorbike "the devil's own horse" and the camera that he used to take pictures "the one-eyed box". Four girls dance the "devil-horse", a youth is selected to play the snake and Lakunle becomes the Traveller. He seeks to be excused to teach Primary Four Geography but Sidi informs him that the village is on holiday due to the arrival of the photographer/traveler.

We also find out that Lakunle made a picture book about the village. There is a picture of Sidi on the front page, and a two-page spread of her somewhere inside. Baroka is featured too, but he "is in a little corner somewhere in the book, and even that corner he shares with one of the village latrines". They banter about for a while, Lakunle gave in and participated because he couldn't tolerate being taunted by them.

The Dance of the Lost Traveller
The four girls crouch on the ground, forming the wheels of the car. Lakunle adjusts their position and sits in air in the middle. He pretends to drive the "car". The four wheels rotate their upper halves of their bodies parallel to the ground in tune with the beat of the drum. The drum beat speeds up to a final crash. The girls dance the stall. They shudder, and drop their faces onto their laps. He pretends to try to restart the "car". He gets out and checks the "wheels" and also pinches them. He tries to start the "car", fails and takes his things for a trek.

He hears a girl singing, but attributes it to sunstroke, so he throws the bottle that he was drinking from in that general direction. He hears a scream and a torrent of abuse. He takes a closer look and sees a girl (played by Sidi). He tries to take photos, but falls down into the stream.

The cast assembles behind him, pretending to be villagers in an ugly mood hauling him to the *odan* tree in the town centre. Then Baroka appears and the play stops. He talks to Lakunle for a while, saying that he knew how the play went and was waiting for the right time to step in. He drops subtle hints of an existing feud between him and Lakunle, then makes the play continue. The villagers once again start thirsting for his blood. He is hauled before Baroka, thrown on his face. He tries to explain his plight. Baroka seems to understand and orders a feast in Lakunle's honour. Lakunle takes the opportunity to take more photos of Sidi. He is also pressed to drink lots of alcohol, and at the end of the play, he is close to vomiting.

The play ends. Sidi praises him for his performance. Lakunle runs away, followed by a flock of women. Baroka and the wrestler sit alone. Baroka takes out his book, and muses that it has been five full months since he last took a wife.

Noon

Sidi is at a road near the market. Lakunle follows her, carrying the firewood that Sidi asks him to help her get. She admires the pictures of her in the magazine. Then Sadiku appears, wearing a shawl over her head. She informs her that the Lion (Baroka) wishes to take her as a wife. Lakunle is outraged, but Sidi stops him. Lakunle changes tactics, telling her as his lover to ignore the message. Sadiku took that as a yes, but Sidi dashed her hopes, saying that since her fame had spread to Lagos and the rest of the world, she deserves more than that. Sadiku presses on, dissembling that Baroka has sworn not to take any more wives after her and that she would be his favourite and would get many privileges, including being able to sleep in the palace rather than one of the outhouses. As Baroka's last wife, she would also be able to become the first, and thus head wife, of his successor, in the same way that Sadiku was Baroka's head wife. However, Sidi sees through her lies, and tells her that she knew that he just wanted fame "as the one man who has possessed 'the jewel of Ilujinle'". Sadiku is flabbergasted and wants to kill Lakunle for what he has done for her.

Sidi shows the magazine. She says that in the picture, she looks absolutely beautiful while he simply looks like a ragged, blackened piece of saddle leather: she is youthful but he is spent. Sadiku changes techniques, saying that if Sidi does not want to be his wife, will she be kind enough to attend a small feast in her honour at his house that night. Sidi refuses, saying that she knows that every woman who has eaten supper with him eventually becomes his wife. Lakunle interjects, informing them that Baroka was known for his wiliness, particularly when he managed to foil the Public Works attempt to build a railroad through Ilujinle. Baroka bribed the surveyor for the route to move the railroad much farther away as "the earth is most unsuitable, could not possibly support the weight of a railway engine". Lakunle is distraught, as he thinks just how close Ilujinle was to civilisation at that time.

The scene cuts to Baroka's bedroom. Ailatu is plucking his armpit hairs. There is a strange machine with a long lever at the side. It is covered with animal skins and rugs. Baroka mentions that she is too soft with her pulls. Then he tells her that he plans to take a new wife, but that he would let her be the "sole out-puller of my sweat-bathed hairs". She is angry, and deliberately plucks the next few hairs a lot harder. Sadiku enters. He shoos Ailatu away, lamenting about his bleeding armpit.

Sadiku informs him that she failed to woo Sidi. She told her that Sidi flatly refused her order, claiming that he was far too old. Baroka pretends to doubt his manliness and asks Sadiku to massage the soles of his feet. Sadiku complies. He lies to her that his manhood ended a week ago, specifically warning her not to tell anyone. He comments that he is only sixty-two. Compared to him, his grandfather had fathered two sons late on sixty-five and Okiki, his father, produced a pair of female twins at sixty-seven. Finally Baroka falls asleep.

Night

Sidi is at the village centre, by the schoolroom window. Enter Sadiku, who is carrying a bundle. She sets down a figure by the tree. She gloats, saying that she has managed to be the undoing (making him impotent) of Baroka, and of his father, Okiki, before that. Sidi is amazed at what she initially perceives to be Sadiku going mad. She shuts the window and exits, shocking Sadiku. After a pause, Sadiku resumes her victory dance and even asks Sidi to join in. Then Lakunle enters. He scorns them, saying that "The full moon is not yet, but the women cannot wait. They must go mad without it." Sidi and Sadiku stop dancing. They talk for a while. As they are about to resume dancing, Sidi states her plans to visit Baroka for his feast and toy with him. Lakunle tries in vain to stop her, telling her that if her deception were to be discovered she would be beaten up. Sidi leaves. Lakunle and Sadiku converse. Lakunle states his grand plans to modernise the area by abolishing the bride-price, building a motor-road through the town and bring city ways to isolated Ilujinle. He goes on to spurn her, calling her a bride-collector for Baroka.

The scene is now Baroka's bedroom. Baroka is arm-wrestling the wrestler seen earlier. He is surprised that she managed to enter unchallenged. Then he suddenly remembers that that day was the designated day off for the servants. He laments that Lakunle had made his servants form an entity called the Palace Workers' Union. He asks if Ailatu was at her usual place, and was disappointed to find out that she had not left him yet despite scolding her severely. Then Sidi mentions that he was here for the supper. Sidi starts playing around with Baroka. She asks him what was up between him and Ailatu. He is annoyed. Changing the subject, Sidi says that she thinks Baroka will win the ongoing arm-wrestling match. Baroka responds humbly, complimenting the strength and ability of the wrestler. She slowly teases Baroka, asking if he was planning to take a wife. She draws an examplee, asking if he was her father, would he let her marry a person like him?

Sidi takes this opportunity to slightly tease him, and is rewarded by his violent reaction by taking the wrestler and slinging him over his shoulder. The wrestler quickly recovers and a new match begins again. The discussion continues. Baroka is hurt by the parallels and subtle hints about his nature dropped by Sidi. Sidi even taunts him, saying that he has failed to produce any children for the last two years. Eventually he is so angered that he slams the wrestler's arm down on the table, winning the match. He tells the defeated wrestler to get the fresh gourd by the door. In the meantime, Baroka tries to paint himself as a grumpy old man with few chances to show his kindliness. The wrestler returns. Baroka continues with his self-glorification. Then he shows her the now-familiar magazine and an addressed envelope. He shows her a stamp, featuring her likeness, and tells her that her picture would adorn the official stamp of the village. The machine at the side of his room is also revealed to be a machine to produce stamps. As she admires the pictures of her in the magazine, Baroka happens to mention that he does not hate progress, only its nature which made "all roofs and faces look the same". He continues praising Sidi's looks, appealing to her.

The scene cuts back to the village centre, where Lakunle is pacing in frustration. He is mad at Sadiku for tricking her to go see Baroka, and at the same time concerned that Baroka will harm or imprison her. Some mummers arrive. Sadiku remains calm, despite Lakunle's growing stress. Sadiku steals a coin from Lakunle to pay the mummers. In return, the mummers drum her praises, but Sadiku claims that Lakunle was the real benefactor. Then they dance the Baroka story, showing him at his prime and his eventual downfall. Lakunle is pleased by the parts where they mock Baroka. Sadiku mentions that she used to be known as Sadiku of the duiker's feet because she could twist and untwist her waist with the smoothness of a water snake.

Sidi appears. She is distraught. Lakunle is outraged, and plans to bring the case to court. Sidi reveals that Baroka only told her at the end that it was a trap. Baroka said that he knew that Sadiku would not keep it to herself, and go out an mock his pride. Lakunle is overcome with emotion, and after at first expressing deep despair, he offers to marry her instead, with no bride-price since she is not a virgin after all. Lakunle is pleased that things have gone as he hoped. Sadiku tells him that Sidi is preparing for a wedding. Lakunle is very happy, saying he needs a day or two to get things ready for a proper Christian wedding. Then musicians appear. Sidi appears, bearing a gift. She tells Lakunle that he is invited to her wedding. Lakunle hopes that the wedding will be between Sidi and himself and her, but she informs her that she has no intention of marrying him, but rather will marry Baroka. Lakunle is stunned. Sidi says that between Baroka and him, at sixty, Baroka is still full of life but Lakunle would be probably "ten years dead". Sadiku then gives Sidi her blessing. The marriage ceremony continues. A young girl taunts Lakunle, and he gives chase. Sadiku gets in his way. He frees himself and clears a space in the crowd for them both to dance.

The drama ends.

Themes

The most prominent theme of this story is the rapid modernisation of Africa, coupled with the rapid evangelisation of the population. This has driven a wedge between the traditionalists, who seek to nullify the changes done in the name of progress due to vested interests or simply not liking the result of progress, and the modernists, who want to see the last of outdated traditional beliefs at all cost.

Another core theme is the marginalisation of women as property. Traditionally, they were seen as properties that could be bought, sold or accumulated. Even the modern Lakunle also falls victim to this, by looking down on Sidi for having a smaller brain and later by wanting to marry her after she lost her virginity since no dowry was required in such a situation

There is also the conflict between education and traditional beliefs. The educated people seek to spread their knowledge to the tribal people in an attempt to make them more modern. This in turn is resisted by the tribal people who see no point in obtaining an education as it served them no use in their daily lives.

Finally, there is the importance of song and dance as a form of spreading information in a world where the fastest route of communication is by foot. It is also an important source of entertainment for the otherwise bored village youths.

Performance

Omonor Imobhio is ideally cast as the beautiful young Sidi, the "Jewel" of the title. She captures perfectly the essence of the uncultured "bush woman" who allows the power of her beauty to go to her head turning her world upside down. But Anthony Ofoegbu is the undoubted star of the show, garnering most of the laughs as the lovestruck modernising schoolteacher. Toyin Oshinaike was impressive as the "Lion" of the title, Baroka, despite struggling with his lines on a couple of occasions and Shola Benjamin was wonderfully comic as the mocking head wife Sadiku. The remainder of the fifteen strong cast, including musicians, all performed admirably.

In general, it was a colourful production with many genuinely funny moments. Despite the generally strong performances however, it has to be said that the direction went somewhat astray with the result that this production fails to capture the acerbic edge of the original play.

Critical reception

The Times Literary Supplement: "In this richly ribald comedy, The Lion and the Jewel, poetry and prose are also blended, but with a marvellous lightness in the treatment of both. The big set-piece of miming in the opening scene, where the villagers re-enact the visit of the white photographer, and the seduction of the village jewel Sidi by the old Lion of a chief, are two of the pinnacles of Mr. Soyinka's achievement to date."

African Forum: "The contemporary theater seems to have forgotten that it has its roots in ritual and song, and it is only the rare emergence of a Lorca or a Brecht-or a Wole Soyinka-that recreates an awareness of our deprivation."

West Africa: "...a brilliant dramatist-the most important in Nigeria, if not in all of Black Africa. He is helped by a profound command of the English language, reflected sometimes in the dazzling brilliance, at other times in the intense poetic quality of his writing...."

The Times Educational Supplement: "He does not use the culture of his ancestors as a gimmick to sell his abilities or even as an export commodity, but as inborn material for expansion. His skilful use of idiom with the lively and musical Nigerian flavour in no way detracts from the command of the English language which he possesses."

The Times, at the time of the play's production at the Royal Court Theatre, London, in December 1966: "This is the third play by Wole Soyinka to appear in London since last year, and this work alone is enough to establish Nigeria as the most fertile new source of English-speaking drama since Synge's discovery of the Western Isles...Even this comparison does Soyinka less than justice, for he is dealing not only with rich folk material, but with the impact of the modern on tribal custom: to find any paralled for his work in English drama you have to go back to the Elizabethans."

Source http://en.wikipedia.org/wiki/The_Lion_and_the_Jewel

The Strong Breed

The Strong Breed is one of the best known plays by Wole Soyinka. It is a tragedy that ends with an individual sacrifice for the sake of the communal benefit. The play is centered on the tradition of egungun, a Yoruba festival tradition in which a scapegoat of the village carries out the evil of the community and is exiled from the civilization. Eman, the play's protagonist, takes on the role of "carrier", knowing it will result in beating and exile. He does this to spare a young simpleton the same fate. The ritual takes an unexpected turn as Eman flees. His pursuers set a trap for him that results in his death.

The play was first published in London in 1964 by Oxford University Press, and subsequently by Rex Collings in 1971.

Navigation menu

Source http://en.wikipedia.org/wiki/The_Strong_Breed

Yoruba Academy

The **Yoruba Academy** is a multi-disciplinary institution that brings together scholars, politicians, businessemen and experts in Yoruba language, culture, economics, law, science and technology, and governance. It was founded in Ibadan, Oyo State, Nigeria in October 2007 following a retreat of young Yoruba professionals, and it is currently operated by the Afenifere Renewal Group. Its main mission is to ensure the preservation of the Yoruba language, as well as the socio-cultural and economic development of the Yoruba peoples worldwide, that is both in its South-West homeland in Nigeria and in the Diaspora.

In its language mission, a dictionary will be maintained by the Academy to set a standard for the Yoruba language.

South-West Yoruba in Nigeria: Ekiti State, Lagos State, Ogun State, Oyo State, Osun State, Ondo State, parts of Kwara State, Kogi State, Edo State, Delta State and Niger State

Diaspora Yoruba outside Nigeria in Africa: in Togo, Benin, Sierra Leone and parts of Ghana

Diaspora Yoruba outside Africa: in Haiti, Cuba, Puerto Rico, Brazil, United States, UK, [(Ireland)]

Source http://en.wikipedia.org/wiki/Yoruba_Academy

Yoruba culture

Yoruba culture refers to the idiosyncratic cultural norms of Yorubaland and the Yoruba people.

Art

Sculpture

The Yoruba are said to be prolific sculptors, famous for their magnificent terra cotta works throughout the 12th and 14th century; artists also harnests their capacity in making artwork out of bronze.

Textile

Weaving is done on different types of looms in order to create hundreds of different patterns.

Cuisine

Yams are said to be one of the important food for the Yoruba; plantain, corn, beans, meat, and fish are also choices.

Naming customs

Yorubas believe that people live out the meanings of their names. As such, Yoruba people put considerable effort into naming a baby. Their philosophy of naming is conveyed in a common adage, *ile ni a n wo, ki a to so omo l'oruko* ("one pays attention to the family before naming a child"): one must consider the tradition and history of a child's relatives when choosing a name.

Some families have long-standing traditions for naming their children. Such customs are often derived from their profession or religion. For example, a family of hunters could name their baby *Ogunbunmi* (Ogun gives me this) to show their respect to the divinity who gives them metal tools for hunting. Meanwhile a family that venerates Ifá may name their child *Falola* (Ifa has honor).

Naming

Since it is generally believed that names are like spirits which would like to live

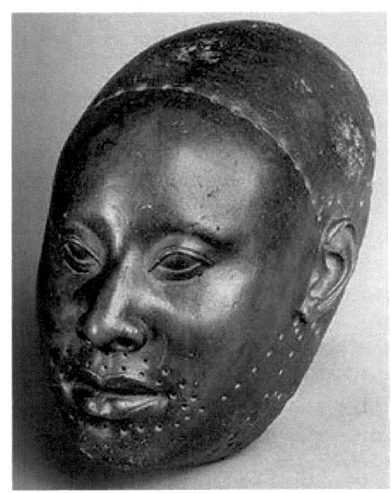
Yoruba bronze head sculpture from the city of Ife, Nigeria c. 12th century A.D

out their meanings, parents do a thorough search before giving names to their babies. Naming ceremonies are performed with this in mind. The oldest family member is given the responsibility of performing the ceremony. Materials used are symbols of the hopes, expectations and prayers of the parents for the new baby. These include honey, kola, bitter kola, atare (alligator pepper), water, palm oil, sugar, sugar cane, salt, and liquor. Each of these has a special meaning in the world-view of the Yoruba. For instance, honey represents sweetness, and the prayer of the parents is that their baby's life will be as sweet as honey.

After the ritual, the child is named and other extended family members are given the honour to give their own names to the child. They do this with gifts of money and clothing. In many cases, they would want to call the child by the name they give him or her. Thus a new baby may end up with more than a dozen names.

Oruko Amutorunwa (Preordained name)

Amutorunwa (brought from heaven)
Oruko - name
Yoruba believe that a baby may come with pre-destined names. For instance, twins (*ibeji*) are believed to have natural-birth names. Thus the first to be born of the two is called *Taiwo* or "Taiye", shortened forms of Taiyewo, meaning the taster of the world. This is to identify the first twin as the one sent by the other one to first go and taste the world. If he/she stays there, it follows that it is not bad, and that would send a signal to the other one to start coming. Hence the second to arrive is named *Kehinde* (late arrival; it is now common for many Kehinde's to be called "Kenny". The child born to the same woman after the twins is called Idowu, and the one after this is called *Alaba* (female) or *Idogbe* (male). *Ige* is a child born with the legs coming out first instead of the head; and *Ojo* (male) or *Aina* (female) is the one born with the umbilical cord around his or her neck. When a child is conceived with no prior menstruation, he or she is named Ilori. *Dada* is the child born with locked hair; and *Ajayi* (nicknamed *Ogidi Olu*) is the one born face-downwards.

Other natural names include *Abiodun* (one born on a festival day or period), *Bosede* (one born on a holy day; *Babatunde/Babatunji* (meaning father has come back) is the son born to a family where a father has recently passed. This testifies to the belief in reincarnation. *Iyabode, Yeside, Yewande, Yetunde,* (mother has come back) is the female counterpart.

Oruko Abiso (Name given at birth)

Oruko - name
Abi - birthed
So - named
These are names that are not natural with the child at birth but are given on either the eight day of birth (for females), and ninth day of birth (for males). They are given in accordance with significant events at time of birth or with reference to the family tradition as has been mentioned above.

Examples of names given with reference to the family tradition include *Ogundiran* (Ogun has become a living tradition in the family); *Ayanlowo* (Ayan drumming tradition is honorable); *Oyetoso* (Chieftaincy is ornament); *Olanrewaju* (Honor is advancing forward); *Olusegun* (God has conquered the enemy).

Abiku Names

Abi - birthed, or Bi - born
Iku - death, or Ku - die / dead
The Yoruba believe that some children are born to die. This derives from the phenomenon of the tragic incidents of high rate of infant mortality sometimes afflicting the same family for a long time. When this occurs, the family devises all kinds of method to forestall a recurrence, including giving special names at a new birth. Such names reflect the frustration of the poor parents: Malomo (do not go again) Kosoko (there is no hoe anymore). This refers to the hoe that is used to dig the grave.
Banjoko (sit with me)
Orukotan (all names have been exhausted)
Yemiitan (stop deceiving me)
Kokumo (this will not die)

Pet names

The Yoruba also have pet names or oriki. These are praise names, and they are used to suggest what the child's family background is or to express one's hope for the child: *Akanbi*- (one who is deliberately born); *Ayinde* (one who is praised on arrival); *Akande* (one who comes or arrives in full determination); *Atanda* (one who is deliberately created after thorough search). For females, *Aduke* (one who everyone likes to bless), Ayoke (one who people are happy to bless), *Arike* (one who is blessed on sight), *Atinuke* or *Abike* (one that is born to be pampered).

Law

Yoruba law is the legal system of Yorubaland. It is quite intricate, each group and subgroup having a system that varies, but in general, government begins within the immediate family. The next level is the clan, or extended family, with its own head known as a Baále. This chief will be subject to town chiefs, and these chiefs are usually themselves subject to their Oba, who may or may not be subject to another Oba himself.

Most of what survived of this legal code has been assimilated into the customary laws of the sovereign nations that the Yoruba inhabit.

Linguistics

Yoruba written literature begins with the formation of its grammar published in 1843. The standard language incorporates several features from other dialects.

Wedding

The child that is named will grow to adulthood. The Yoruba culture provides for the upbringing of the child by the extended family. In traditional society, the child is placed with a master of whatever craft the gods specify for him or her. Or he may take to the profession of the father, in the case of a boy, or the mother, in the case of a girl. The parents have the responsibility for his/her socialization into the norms of the larger society, in addition to giving him a means of livelihood. His or her wedding is also the responsibility of the parents.

The wedding ceremony is the climax of a process that starts with courtship. The young man identifies a young woman that he loves. He and his friends seek her out through various means, including playing pranks. The young man sends messages of interest to the young woman, until such a time that they are close enough to avoid a go-between (alarina). Then once they both express mutual love, they let their parents know about their feelings for each other. The man's parents arrange to pay a visit to the prospective bride's parents. Once their consent is secured, the wedding day may be set. Prior to the wedding day, the payment of bride price is arranged. This secures the final consent of the bride's parents, and the wedding day is fixed. Once the day has been fixed through consultation with the Orisa, the bride and bridegroom are warned to avoid travelling out of town, including to the farm. This is to prevent any mishap. The wedding day is a day of celebration, eating, drinking and dancing for parents, relations, the new husband and wife and their friends and, often, even foes. Marriage is not considered to be only a union of the husband and wife, it is also seen among the Yoruba as the union of the families on both sides. But before the bride goes to her husbands house, she is escorted by different people i.e. family and friends to the door step of her new home. There she is prayed for and her legs are washed. It is believed that she is washing every bad-luck that she might have brought into her husband's house away. Before she is finally ushered into her house, she is given a calabash (igba) and then she is asked to break it. When it breaks, the amount of pieces it is broken into is believed to be the number of children she will give birth to. On the wedding night she and her husband have their first meeting and he is ordinarily expected to find her to be a virgin. If he doesn't, she and her parents are disgraced and may be banished from the village where they live.

Music

Music and dance have always been an important part of their culture; used in the many different forms of entertainment.

Funeral

In Yoruba thought, death is not the end of life; it is rather a transition from one form of existence to another. The ogberis (ignorant folks) fear death because it marks the end of an existence that is known and the beginning of one that is unknown. Immortality is the dream of many, as "Eji-ogbe" puts it: *Mo dogbogbo orose; Ng ko ku mo; Mo digba oke; Mo le gboin.* (I have become an aged ose tree; I will no longer die; I have become two hundred hills rolled into one; I am immovable.)

The Yoruba also pray for many blessings, but the most important three are wealth, children and immortality: ire owo; ire omo; ire aiku pari iwa. There is a belief in an afterlife that is a continuation of this life, only in a different setting, and the abode of the dead is usually placed at a place just outside of this abode, and is sometimes thought of as separated by a stream. Participation in this afterlife is conditional on the nature of one's life and the nature of one's death. This is the meaning of life: to deliver the message of Olodumare, the Supreme Creator by promoting the good of existence. For it is the wish of the Deity that human beings should promote the good as much as is possible. Hence it is insisted that one has a good capacity for moral uprightness and personhood. Personhood is an achieved state judged by the standard of goodness to self, to the community and to the ancestors. As people say: *Keni huwa gbedegbede; keni lee ku pelepele; K'omo eni lee n'owo gbogboro L'eni sin.* (Let one conduct one' life gently; that one may die a good death; that one's children may stretch their hands over one's body in burial.)

The achievement of a good death is an occasion for celebration of the life of the deceased. This falls into several categories. First, children and grand children would celebrate the life of their parent who passed and left a good name for them. Second, the Yoruba are realistic and pragmatic about their attitude to death. They know that one may die at a young age. The important thing is a good life and a good name. As the saying goes: *Ki a ku l'omode, ki a fi esin se irele eni; o san ju ki a dagba ki a ma ni adie irana.* (if we die young, and a horse is killed in celebration of one's life; it is better than dying old without people killing even a chicken in celebration.)

It is also believed that ancestors have enormous power to watch over their descendants. Therefore, people make an effort to remember their ancestors on a regular basis. This is ancestor veneration, which some have wrongly labelled ancestor worship. It is believed that the love that exists between a parent and a child here on earth should continue even after death. And since the parent has only ascended to another plane of existence, it should be possible for the link to remain strong.

Philosophy

Yoruba culture consists of folk/cultural philosophy, religion and literature. They are embodied in Ifa-Ife Divination, known as the tripartite Book of Enlightenment in Yorubaland and in Diaspora.

Yoruba philosophy is a witness of two epochs. The first epoch is an epoch-making history in cosmology and mythology. This is also an epoch-making history in oral philosophy in oral culture during which time Oduduwa was the sole philosopher, the head, and a pre-eminent diviner. He theorized about the visible and invisible worlds, reminiscing about the cosmology, cosmogony, and the mythological creatures in the visible and invisible worlds.

The second epoch is the epoch of metaphysical philosophy. This commenced in the 19th century when the land has become a literate land through the diligence and pragmatism of Dr. Bishop Ajayi Crowther, the first Anglican African Bishop.

Yoruba philosophy is mainly a narrative philosophy, explicating and pointing to the knowledge of the causes and the nature of things, affecting the corporeal and the spiritual universe and its wellness. Yoruba people have hundreds of philosophical aphorisms and lores, and they believe that any lore that widens people's horizons and presents food for thought is the beginning of philosophy.

Although religion is often considered first in Yoruba culture, nonetheless it is philosophy, the thought of man and the resoning of the mind that actually leads the faculty (ori) to the creation and the practice of religion. Thus philosophy is antecedent to religion.

Today, the academic and nonacademic people are becoming more and more interested in Yoruba philosophy. Thus more and more researches are being carried out on Yoruba philosophy, as more and more books are being written on it—to emboss its contemporary mark and to advance its research amongst non-African thinkers and political scientists who are beginning to open their doors to other cultures, thus widening their views.

Religion

The Yoruba are said to be religious people, but they are also pragmatic and tolerant about their religious differences. Whilst many profess the Yoruba school of thought; many profess other faiths e.g. Christianity, Islam, Budhism, Hinduism e.t.c.

Language

Yoruba people traditionally speak the Yorùbá language, a member of the Niger–Congo language family. Apart from referring to the aggregate of dialects and their speakers, the term Yoruba is used for the standard, written form of the language.

Source http://en.wikipedia.org/wiki/Yoruba_culture

Yoruba language

Yorùbá	
èdè Yorùbá	
Spoken natively in	Nigeria, Togo, Benin
Ethnicity	Yoruba people
Native speakers	28 million (2007)
Language family	Niger–Congo
	Atlantic–Congo
	Volta–Niger
	YEAI
	Yoruboid
	Edekiri
	Yorùbá
Writing system	Latin
Official status	
Official language in	Nigeria
Language codes	
ISO 639-1	yo
ISO 639-2	yor
ISO 639-3	yor

The **Yoruba language** (natively èdè Yorùbá) is a Niger–Congo language spoken in West Africa. The number of speakers of Yoruba was estimated at around 20 million in the 1990s. The native tongue of the Yoruba people, is spoken, among other languages, in Nigeria, Benin, and Togo and in communities in other parts of Africa, Europe and the Americas. A variety of the language, Lucumi, from olukunmi is used as the liturgical language of the Santeria religion of Cuba, Puerto Rico, Dominican Republic and the United States. It is most closely related to the Owo and Itsekiri language (spoken in the Niger-Delta) and Igala spoken in central Nigeria.

History

Yoruba is classified within the Edekiri languages, which together with Itsekiri and the isolate Igala form the Yoruboid group of languages within the Volta-Niger branch of the Niger-Congo phylum. The linguistic unity of the Niger-Congo phylum dates to deep prehistory, estimates ranging around 15 kya (the end of the Upper Paleolithic). The Atlantic–Congo core of this group would have formed roughly 8,000 years ago. The Benue-Congo branch (which also includes the Bantoid branch) separated from Atlantic-Congo around the 5th millennium BC, ultimately spreading out in the Bantu expansion, while Volta-Niger is one of the branches formed by the peoples who remained in the Atlantic-Congo core territory.

The Yoruba group are assumed to have developed out of undifferentiated Volta–Niger populations by the 1st millennium BC. Settlements of early Yoruba speakers are assumed to correspond to those found in the wider Niger area from about the 4th century BC, especially at Ife. As the North-West Yoruba dialects show more linguistic innovation, combined with the fact that Southeast and Central Yoruba areas generally have older settlements, suggests a later date of immigration for Northwest Yoruba.

Varieties

The Yoruba dialect continuum itself consists of several dialects. The various Yoruba dialects in the Yorubaland of Nigeria can be classified into three major dialect areas: Northwest, Central, and Southeast. Of course, clear boundaries can never be drawn and peripheral areas of dialectal regions often have some similarities to adjoining dialects.

North-West Yoruba (NWY).
Abẹokuta, Ibadan, Ọyọ, Ogun and Lagos (Eko) areas

Central Yoruba (CY)
Igbomina, Yagba, Ilésà, Ifẹ, Ekiti,

Akurẹ, Ẹfọn, and Ijẹbu areas.
South-East Yoruba (SEY)
Okitipupa, Ilaje, Ondo, Ọwọ, Ikarẹ, Ṣagamu, and parts of Ijẹbu.

North-West Yoruba is historically a part of the Ọyọ empire. In NWY dialects, Proto-Yoruba /gh/ (the velar fricative [ɣ]) and /gw/ have merged into /w/; the upper vowels /i̩/ and /u̩/ were raised and merged with /i/ and /u/, just as their nasal counterparts, resulting in a vowel system with seven oral and three nasal vowels. Ethnographically, traditional government is based on a division of power between civil and war chiefs; lineage and descent are unilineal and agnatic.

South-East Yoruba was probably associated with the expansion of the Benin Empire after c. 1450 AD. In contrast to NWY, lineage and descent are largely multilineal and cognatic, and the division of titles into war and civil is unknown. Linguistically, SEY has retained the /gh/ and /gw/ contrast, while it has lowered the nasal vowels /i̩n/ and /u̩n/ to /ẹn/ and /ọn/, respectively. SEY has collapsed the second and third person plural pronominal forms; thus, *àn án wá* can mean either 'you (pl.) came' or 'they came' in SEY dialects, whereas NWY for example has *ẹ wá* 'you (pl.) came' and *wọ́n wá* 'they came', respectively. The emergence of a plural of respect may have prevented coalescence of the two in NWY dialects.

Central Yoruba forms a transitional area in that the lexicon has much in common with NWY, whereas it shares many ethnographical features with SEY. Its vowel system is the least innovating (most stable) of the three dialect groups, having retained nine oral-vowel contrasts and six or seven nasal vowels, and an extensive vowel harmony system.

Literary Yoruba

Literary Yoruba, also known as *Standard Yoruba*, *Yoruba koiné*, and *common Yoruba*, is a separate member of the dialect cluster. It is the written form of the language, the standard variety learned at school and that spoken by newsreaders on the radio. Standard Yoruba has its origin in the 1850s, when Samuel A. Crowther, the first African Bishop, published a Yoruba grammar and started his translation of the Bible. Though for a large part based on the Ọyọ and Ibadan dialects, Standard Yoruba incorporates several features from other dialects. It also has some features peculiar to itself, for example the simplified vowel harmony system, as well as foreign structures, such as calques from English which originated in early translations of religious works.

Because the use of Standard Yoruba did not result from some deliberate linguistic policy, much controversy exists as to what constitutes 'genuine Yoruba', with some writers holding the opinion that the Ọyọ dialect is the most "pure" form, and others stating that there is no such thing as genuine Yoruba at all. Standard Yoruba, the variety learnt at school and used in the media, has nonetheless been a powerful consolidating factor in the emergence of a common Yoruba identity.

Writing system

In the 17th century Yoruba was written in the Ajami script, a form of Arabic. Modern Yoruba orthography originated in the early work of CMS missionaries working among the *Aku* (Yoruba) of Freetown. One of their informants was Crowther, who later would proceed to work on his native language himself. In early grammar primers and translations of portions of the English Bible, Crowther used the Latin alphabet largely without tone markings. The only diacritic used was a dot below certain vowels to signify their open variants [ɛ] and [ɔ], viz. ⟨ẹ⟩ and ⟨ọ⟩. Over the years the orthography was revised to represent tone among other things. In 1875 the Church Missionary Society (CMS) organised a conference on Yoruba Orthography; the standard devised there was the basis for the orthography of the steady flow of religious and educational literature over the next seventy years.

The current orthography of Yoruba derives from a 1966 report of the Yoruba Orthography Committee, along with Ayọ Bamgboṣe's 1965 *Yoruba Orthography*, a study of the earlier orthographies and an attempt to bring Yoruba orthography in line with actual speech as much as possible. Still largely similar to the older orthography, it employs the Latin alphabet modified by the use of the digraph ⟨gb⟩ and certain diacritics, including the traditional vertical line set under the letters ⟨ẹ⟩, ⟨ọ⟩, and ⟨ṣ⟩. In many publications the line is replaced by a dot ⟨ẹ⟩, ⟨ọ⟩, ⟨ṣ⟩. The vertical line had been used to avoid the mark being fully covered by an underline.

A B D E Ẹ F G Gb H I J K L M
a b d e ẹ f g gb h i j k l m
The Latin letters ⟨c⟩, ⟨q⟩, ⟨v⟩, ⟨x⟩, ⟨z⟩ are not used.

The pronunciation of the letters without diacritics corresponds more or less to their International Phonetic Alphabet equivalents, except for the labial-velar stops [k͡p] (written ⟨p⟩) and [g͡b] (written ⟨gb⟩), in which both consonants are pronounced simultaneously rather than sequentially. The diacritic underneath vowels indicates an open vowel, pronounced with the root of the tongue retracted (so ⟨ẹ⟩ is pronounced [ɛ] and ⟨ọ⟩ is [ɔ]). ⟨ṣ⟩ represents a postalveolar consonant [ʃ] like the English ⟨sh⟩, ⟨y⟩ represents a palatal approximant like English ⟨y⟩, and ⟨j⟩ a voiced palatal plosive, as is common in many African orthographies.

In addition to the vertical bars, three further diacritics are used on vowels and syllabic nasal consonants to indicate the language's tones: an acute accent ⟨´⟩ for the high tone, a grave accent ⟨`⟩ for the low tone, and an optional macron ⟨¯⟩ for the middle tone. These are used in addition to the line in ⟨ẹ⟩ and ⟨ọ⟩. When more than one tone is used in one syllable, the vowel can either be written once for each tone (for example, *⟨òó⟩ for a vowel [o] with tone rising from low to high) or, more rarely in current usage, combined into a single accent. In this case, a caron ⟨ˇ⟩ is used for the rising tone (so the previous example would be written ⟨ǒ⟩) and a circumflex ⟨^⟩ for the falling tone.

Á À Ā É È Ē Ẹ Ẹ́ Ẹ̀ Ẹ̄ Í Ì Ī Ó
Ẹ Ẹ́ Ẹ̀ Ẹ̄

á à ā é è ē ẹ ẹ́ ẹ̀ ẹ̄ í ì ī ó ò
ẹ ẹ́ ẹ̀ ẹ̄

In Benin, Yoruba uses a different orthography. The Yoruba alphabet was standardized along with other Benin languages in the National Languages Alphabet by the National Language Commission in 1975, and revised in 1990 by the National Center for Applied Linguistics.

A B D E Ɛ F G Gb H I J K KP L
a b d e ɛ f g gb h i j k kp l

Linguistic features

Phonology

The three possible syllable structures of Yoruba are consonant+vowel (CV), vowel alone (V), and syllabic nasal (N). Every syllable bears one of the three tones: high ⟨ó⟩, mid ⟨o⟩ (generally left unmarked), and low ⟨ò⟩. The sentence 'ń ò lọ' *I didn't go* provides examples of the three syllable types:

ń — [ŋ̄] — *I*
ò — [ó] — *not* (negation)
lọ — [lɔ] — *to go*

Vowels

Standard Yoruba has seven oral and five nasal vowels. There are no diphthongs in Yoruba; sequences of vowels are pronounced as separate syllables. Dialects differ in the number of vowels they have; see above.

	Oral vowels		Nasal vowels	
	Front	Back	Front	Back
Close	i	u	ĩ	ũ
Close-mid	e	o		
Open-mid	ɛ	ɔ	ɛ̃	ɔ̃
Open	a			

The status of a fifth nasal vowel, [ã], is controversial. Although the sound does occur in speech, several authors have argued it to be not phonemically contrastive; often, it is in free variation with [ɔ̃]. Orthographically, nasal vowels are normally represented by an oral vowel symbol followed by ⟨n⟩ (i.e., ⟨in⟩, ⟨un⟩, ⟨ẹn⟩, ⟨ọn⟩), except in case of the [n] allophone of /l/ (see below) preceding a nasal vowel, i.e. *inú* 'inside, belly' is actually pronounced [īnű].

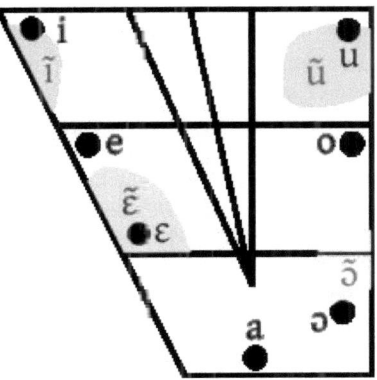

Yoruba vowel diagram. Oral vowels are marked by black dots, while the coloured regions indicate the ranges in possible quality of the nasal vowels.

Consonants

	Labial	Alveolar	Postalveolar/Palatal
Nasal	m		
Plosive	b	t d	ɟ
Fricative	f	s	ʃ
Approximant		l ~ n	j
Rhotic		r	

The voiceless plosives /t/ and /k/ are slightly aspirated; in some Yoruba varieties, /t/ and /d/ are more dental. The rhotic consonant is realized as a flap [ɾ], or in some varieties (notably Lagos Yoruba) as the alveolar approximant [ɹ]. Like many other languages of the region, Yoruba has the labial-velar stops /k͡p/ and /ɡ͡b/, e.g. *pápá* [k͡pák͡pá] 'field', *gbọ̄gbọ̄* [ɡbɔɡbɔ] 'all'. Notably, it lacks the common voiceless bilabial plosive /p/, which is why /k͡p/ is written as ⟨p⟩. It also lacks a phoneme /n/; though the letter ⟨n⟩ is used for the sound in the orthography, it strictly speaking refers to an allophone of /l/ which immediately precedes a nasal vowel.

There is also a syllabic nasal which forms a syllable nucleus by itself. When it precedes a vowel it is a velar nasal [ŋ], e.g. *n ò lọ* [ŋ ò lɔ] 'I didn't go'. In other cases its place of articulation is homorganic with the following consonant, for example *ó ń lọ* [ó ń lɔ] 'he is going', *ó ń fò* [ó ḿ fò] 'he is jumping'.

Tone

Yoruba is a tonal language with three level tones: high, low, and mid (the default tone.) Every syllable must have at least one tone; a syllable containing a long vowel can have two tones. Contour tones (i.e. rising or falling tone melodies) are usually analysed as separate tones occurring on adjacent tone bearing units (morae) and thus have no phonemic status. Tones are marked by use of the acute accent for high tone (⟨á⟩, ⟨ń⟩), the grave accent for low tone (⟨à⟩, ⟨ǹ⟩); Mid is unmarked, except on syllabic nasals where it is indicated using a macron (⟨a⟩, ⟨n̄⟩); see below). Examples:

H: ó bẹ́ 'he jumped'; síbí 'spoon'
M: ó bẹ 'he is forward'; ara 'body'
L: ó bẹ̀ 'he asks for pardon'; ọ̀kọ̀ 'spear'.

Assimilation and elision

When a word precedes another word beginning with a vowel, assimilation or deletion ('elision') of one of the vowels often takes place. In fact, since syllables in Yoruba normally end in a vowel, and most nouns start with one, this is a very common phenomenon, and indeed only is absent in very slow, unnatural speech. The orthography here follows speech in that word divisions are normally not indicated in words that are contracted as a result of assimilation or elision: *ra ẹja* → *rẹja* 'buy fish'. Sometimes however, authors may choose to use an inverted comma to indicate an elided vowel as in *ní ilé* → *n'ílé* 'in the house'.

Long vowels within words usually signal that a consonant has been elided word-internally. In such cases, the tone of the elided vowel is retained, e.g. *àdirò* → *ààrò* 'hearth'; *koríko* → *koóko* 'grass'; *òtító* → *òótó* 'truth'.

Grammar

Yoruba is a highly isolating language, with an index of synthesis of 1.09. Its basic constituent order is subject–verb–object (SVO), as in *ó nà Adé* 'he beat Adé'. The bare verb stem denotes a completed action (often called perfect); tense and aspect are marked by preverbal particles such as *ń* 'imperfect/present continuous', *ti* 'past'. Negation is expressed by a preverbal particle *kò*. Serial verb constructions are common, as in many other languages of West Africa.

Although Yoruba has no grammatical gender, it does have a distinction between human and non-human nouns; probably a remainder of the noun class system of proto-Niger–Congo, the distinction is only apparent in the fact that the two groups require different interrogative particles: *tani* for human nouns ('who?') and *kini* for non-human nouns ('what?'). The associative construction (covering possessive/genitive and related notions) consists of juxtaposing nouns in the order modified-modifier as in *inú àpótí* {inside box} 'the inside of the box', *filà Àkàndé* 'Akande's cap' or *àpótí aṣọ* 'box for clothes' (Bamgboṣe 1966:110, Rowlands 1969:45-6). More than two nouns can be juxtaposed: *rélùweè abẹ́ ilẹ̀* (railway under ground) 'underground railway', *inú àpótí aṣọ* 'the inside of the clothes box'. In the rare case where this results in two possible readings, disambiguation is left to the context. Plural nouns are indicated by a plural word.

There are two 'prepositions': *ní* 'on, at, in' and *sí* 'onto, towards'. The former indicates location and absence of movement, the latter encodes location/direction with movement (Sachnine 1997:19). Position and direction are expressed by these prepositions in combination with spatial relational nouns like *orí* 'top', *apá* 'side', *inú* 'inside', *etí* 'edge', *abẹ́* 'under', *ilẹ̀* 'down', etc. Many of these spatial relational terms are historically related to body-part terms.

Loanwords

Modern Yoruba has loanwords from diverse sources, including Islamic religious and Western cultural terms. From Arabic come *adua/adura* "prayer", "supplication" الدعاء *ad-du'a*; *sanma*, "heaven", "sky", السماء *samaa`*; *Jimoh*, "Friday", الجمعة *Al-Jum'ah*. Some of a large number of loans from English include: *alaamu*, "alarm"; *baagu*, "bag"; *baafu*, "bath"; *gaseeti*, "gazette"; *baati*, "bat"; *siiki*, "sick"; *risiiti*, receipt.

Source http://en.wikipedia.org/wiki/Yoruba_language

Yoruba literature

Yoruba literature is the spoken and written literature of the Yoruba people, the largest ethno-linguistic group in Nigeria, and in Africa. The Yorùbá language is spoken in Nigeria, Benin, and Togo, as well as in dispersed Yoruba communities throughout the world.

Writing

Yoruba did not have a common written form before the nineteenth century. Many of the early contributions to Yoruba writing and formal study were made by English-educated Anglican priests. The first Yoruba grammar was published in 1843 by Bishop Samuel Ajayi Crowther. He himself was of Yoruba origin. The written form of the Yoruba language comes from a Conference on Orthography from the Church Missionary Society in Lagos, in 1875. The first history of the Yoruba people was compiled by Reverend Samuel Johnson in 1897 who was also of Yoruba origin. Thus, the formation of written Yoruba was facilitated by Yoruba people themselves despite the use of the Roman alphabet.

Mythology

Yoruba religion is intertwined with history, with Yoruba claiming to descend from divinities, and some kings becoming deified after their deaths. *Itan* is the word for the sum of Yoruba religion, poetry, song, and history. Yoruba divinities are called Orishas, and make up one of the most complex pantheons in oral history.

Ifá, a complex system of divination, involves recital of Yoruba poetry containing stories and proverbs bearing on the divination. A divination recital can take a whole night. The body of this poetry is vast, and passed on between Ifa oracles.

Fiction

The first novel in the Yorùbá language was *Ogboju Ode ninu Igbo Irunmale* (*The Forest of A Thousand Demons*), written in 1938 by Chief Daniel O. Fagunwa (1903–1963). It contains the picaresque tales of a Yoruba hunter encountering folklore elements, such as magic, monsters, spirits, and gods. It was one of the first novels to be written in any African language. Fagunwa wrote other works based on similar themes, and remains the most widely-read Yorùbá-language author.

Amos Tutuola (1920–1997) was greatly inspired by Fagunwa, but wrote in an intentionally rambling, broken English, reflecting the oral tradition. Tutuola gained fame for *The Palm-Wine Drinkard* (1946, pub 1952), and other works based on Yoruba folklore.

Senator Afolabi Olabimtan (1932–1992) was a writer, along with professor, and politician. He wrote Yoruba language novels about modern Nigerian life and love, such as *Kekere Ekun* (1967; *[Lad Nicknamed] Leopard Cub*), and *Ayanmo* (1973; *Predestination*).

Theatre

In his pioneering study of Yoruba theatre, Joel Adedeji traced its origins to the masquerade of the Egungun (the "cult of the ancestor"). The traditional rite is controlled exclusively by men and culminates in a masquerade in which ancestors return to the world of the living to visit their descendants. In addition to its origin in ritual, Yoruba theatre can be "traced to the 'theatrogenic' nature of a number of the deities in the Yoruba pantheon, such as Obatala the god of creation, Ogun the god of creativeness and Sango the god of lightning", whose worship is imbricated "with drama and theatre and their symbolic and psychological uses."

The Aláàrìnjó theatrical tradition sprang from the Egungun masquerade. The Aláàrìnjó were a troupe of traveling performers who were masked (as were the participants in the Egungun rite).

They created short, satirical scenes that drew on a number of established stereotypical characters. Their performances used mime, music and acrobatics. The Aláàrìnjó tradition influenced the Yoruba traveling theatre, which was the most prevalent and highly developed form of theatre in Nigeria from the 1950s to the 1980s. In the 1990s, the Yoruba traveling theatre moved into television and film and now gives live performances only rarely.

"Total theatre" also developed in Nigeria in the 1950s. It used non-Naturalistic techniques, surrealistic physical imagery, and exercised a flexibile use of language. Playwrights writing in the mid 1970s made use of some of these techniques, but articulated them with "a radical appreciation of the problems of society."

Traditional performance modes have strongly influenced the major figures in contemporary Nigerian theatre. The work of Hubert Ogunde (sometimes referred to as the "father of contemporary Yoruban theatre") was informed by the Aláàrìnjó tradition and Egungun masquerades. He founded the first professional Nigerian theatre company in 1945 and served in many roles, including playwright, in both English and Yoruba.

Wole Soyinka is "generally recognized as Africa's greatest living playwright" and was awarded the 1986 Nobel Prize in Literature. He writes in English, sometimes a Nigerian pidgin English, and his subjects (in both plays and novels) include a mixture of Western, traditional, and modern African elements. He gives the god Ogun a complex metaphysical significance in his work. In his essay "The Fourth Stage" (1973), Soyinka argues that "no matter how strongly African authors call for an indigenous tragic art form, they smuggle into their dramas, through the back door of formalistic and ideological predilections, typically conventional Western notions and practices of rendering historical events into tragedy." He contrasts Yoruban drama with classical Athenian drama, relating both to the 19th-century German philosopher Friedrich Nietzsche's analysis of the latter in *The Birth of Tragedy* (1879). Ogun, he argues, is "a totality of the Dionysian, Apollonian and Promethean virtues." He develops an aesthetic of Yoruban tragedy based, in part, on the Yoruban religious pantheon (including Ogun and Obatala).

Akinwunmi Isola is a popular novelist (beginning with *O Le Ku, Heart-Reading Incidents*, in 1974), playwright, screenwriter, film producer, and professor of Yoruba language. His works include historical dramas and analyses of modern Yoruba novels.

Source http://en.wikipedia.org/wiki/Yoruba_literature

Yoruba medicine

Yorùbá medicine (egbogi) is a herbal-based form of the science and art of healing. This form of herbal medicine is embraced by various communities in West Africa, the Caribbean and elsewhere around the globe.

"African herbal medicine is commonly called Yorubic or Orisha medicine on the African continent. It started from a religious text, called Ifa Corpus. According to tradition, the Ifa Corpus was revealed by the mystic prophet, Orunmilla, around 4,000 years ago in the ancient city of Ile-Ife, now known as major city in Yorùbáland. The last 400 years saw individuals in the Caribbean and South America practice the Yorubic healing system as a token of their past when the first wave of personnel arrived in the Americas.

Herbal medicine, also called botanical medicine or phytomedicine, refers to the use of any plant's seeds, berries, roots, leaves, bark, or flowers for medicinal purposes.

Basic Philosophies

According to A D Buckley, Yorùbá medicine has major similarities to conventional medicine in the sense that its main thrust is to kill or expel from the body tiny, invisible "germs" or insects (*kokoro*) and also worms (*aron*) which inhabit small bags within the body. For the Yoruba, however, these germs and worms perform useful functions in the healthy body, aiding digestion, fertility etc. However, if they become too powerful in the body, they must be controlled, killed or driven out with bitter-tasting plants contained in medicines. Yorùbá medicine is quite different from homeopathy, which uses medicinal ingredients that imitates pathological symptoms. Rather, in a similar manner to mainstream European medicine, it strives to destroy the agencies that cause disease.

Buckley claims that traditional Yorùbá ideas of the human body are derived from the image of a cooking pot, susceptible to overflowing. The female body overflows dangerously but necessarily once a month; germs and worms in the body can overflow their "bags" in the body if they are given too much "sweet" (tasty) food. The household is understood in a similar way. As germs overflow their bag, menstrual blood the female body, and palm oil the cooking pot, so women in the marital household tend to overflow and return to their natal homes.

As well as using bitter plants to kill germs and worms, Yorùbá herbalists also use incantation (*ofo*) in medicines to bring good luck (*awure*), for example, to bring money or love. Medicinal incantations are in some ways like the praise songs addressed to human beings or gods: their purpose is to awaken the power of the ingredients hidden in the medicine. Most medicinal incantations use a form of word-play, similar to punning, to evoke the properties of the plants implied by the name of the plant.

Some early writers believed that the Yoruba people are actually an East African tribe who moved from the Nile River to the Niger area. For example, Dr. Jonathan Olumide Lucas claims that "the Yoruba, during antiquity, lived in ancient Egypt before migrating to the Atlantic coast."

"With Egypt at its roots, it is therefore inevitable that African herbal medicine became associated with magic. Amulets and charms were more common than pills as preventions or curatives of diseases. Priests, who were from the earliest days the forefathers of science and medicine, considered diseases as possession by evil demons and could be treated using incantations along with extracts from the roots of certain plants. The psychosomatic method of healing disorders used primarily by psychiatrists today is based loosely on this ancient custom."

Yorùbá traditionalists claim in their oratory history that Orunmilla taught the people the customs of divination, prayer, dance, symbolic gestures, personal, and communal elevation. They believe he also advised his people on spiritual baths, meditation, and herbal medicine in particular. The Ifa Corpus is considered to be the foundation of the traditionalist herbology.

Deliberation

To the modern man/woman, some medicinal practices may be deemed to be a bit too weird for their liking. But it must be recognized that to the Yorùbás it is not merely a procedure such as it is in other forms, but an outright system. Sometimes referred to as a remedy, a religious undertone and a scientific phenomenon all rolled into one.°

Controversy

Integration

Oyelakin suggests that the major difference between **Yorùbá medicine** and orthodox medicine is that the former is homeopathic in nature while the later is allopathic.

He goes on to say that the orthodox methodology for the treatment of diseases is based on what he called "the contrary principle"
which states that: *illnesses and diseases should be treated with chemical agents that produce effects that are in opposition to those exhibited by the illnesses being treated.*
This type of practise is also concerned primarily with the elimination of symptoms. However, according to **Makinde**:
The treatment of a disease is the application of what such disease is forbidden to come in contact with, at whose sight must simply disappear
Furthermore, while allopathic medicine is preoccupied with getting rid of the symptoms, homeopathic medicine is more concerned with identifying the causes of the illness and disease in an effort to restore **holistic balance** in the biological system.

This suggests that while orthodox medicine is only occupied with one function;
Getting rid of the symptoms,
Yorùbá medicine performs three distinct functions:
Getting rid of the symptoms,
Identifying and removing the causes of the illness, and
Maintaining a holistic balance in the patient.
It has been argued that it is untrue the claims that suggest orthodox medicine is not concerned with identifying and removing the causes of illness. Like for instance STD and the warning against casual intercourse.

Holistic Health

Even though the above argument cannot be used in terms of the holistic healing of a patient, modern orthodox medicine has a place for this concept whereby all aspects of the patients needs, psychological, physical and social, and mentally are said to be taken into account and seen as a whole. Yet this barely "scratches the surface" if compared to the Yorubas viewpoint as does include this concept and further divulges into other aspects in terms of the patients emotional, spiritual, and even environmental balance/imbalance.

In his piece on "Yorùbá Culture" **Kola Abimbola** stipulates that in order to achieve a holistic healing through Yorùbá medicine, some certain conditions must hold. For instance, the Onisegun (Herbalist) would be interested in the spiritual causes of the illness. To do this, there is the need for the understanding of the constitution of man. For him, a person has two parts which he describes as "the body" and "the soul complex".

"Taking into account one's body, mind, emotions, and spiritual life, holistic health combines the best of modern diagnosis and monitoring techniques with both ancient and innovative health methods. These can include natural diet and herbal remedies, nutritional supplements, exercise, relaxation, psychospiritual counseling, meditation, breathing exercises, and other self-regulatory practices. It addresses not only symptoms, but the entire person, and his or her current life predicament, including family, job, and religious life. It emphasizes prevention, health maintenance, high-level wellness and longevity. It views the client as an active participant in the healing process, rather than simply a passive recipient of "health care." At once personal, ecological, and transcultural, holism has become the new health paradigm for the 21st century."

Orishas in Yorùbá Medicine

Tradition has it that many Orishas (deities/divinities) play a significant role in the life of the Yorùbás nevertheless in this form of medicine. And with this "Osanyin/Osain" or 'the whispering genie' is deemed one of the more important.

Osain is associated with the domination over all wild herbs, and is considered by most practitioners as the greatest herbalist that ever lived. There are so many herbs and plants that can be used in healing, that only someone with a "trained eyed" can take full advantage of their functions. For instance, a stipulation of concession has it that although plants and herbs have purely their "medicinal value", they also carry "mystical value".

The "Osainista" is said to be an expert in local herbology; possessing the "know how" on herbs and plants; correctly gathering the necessary herbs and plants for the right cause. Some plants are to be gathered at certain times of the day or night. Certain plants are meant to be exposed to the necessary incantation(s) and implementation of offerings in order to reap adequate results. As said before there are a multitude of Orisha's each with their physical qualities and herbal attributes, each sometimes interwoven into one another.

Ifa has been said to also play an important role towards achieving the end product of any one healing process.

Orishas	Attributes	Physical Correspondence
Orunmila	Yorùbá Grand Priest and custodian of the Ifa Oracle, source of knowledge is believed to have good knowledge of Human Form, Purity, Cures illness and deformities. His suburdinate priests or followers are the Babalawo.	Skullcap, Sage, Kola Nut, Basil, Hyssop, Blue Vervain, White Willow, Valerian
Èsù or Elegbara	Often ill-translated as "The Devil" or "The Evil Being", Èsù is neither of these but best referred to as "The Trickster" dealing a hand of misfortune to those that do not tribute or deemed to be constantly "unaware" of their surroundings. Also referred as "divine messenger"; a prime negotiator between negative and positive forces in body; enforcer of the "law of being". And is said to assist in enhancing the power derived from herbal medicines.	sympathetic nervous system
Ogún	The divinity of iron and metalurgy.	heart, kidney (adrenal glands) tendons, and sinews
Yemoja	Literarily Mother Fish is held by Yoruba traditionalists as Mother of Waters, Nurturer of Water Resources. According to Olorishas, she is the amniotic fluid in the womb of the pregnant woman, as well as, the breasts which nurture. She is considered the protective energies of the feminine force.	womb, liver, breasts, buttocks
Oshun	Wife of former Oba of Oyo called Shango (another Yoruba Orisha see below) is said to turn into a river in Osogbo. Yoruba historians ascribed to her Sensuality, Beauty, Gracefulness, symbolizing Yorubas' search for clarity and flowing motion. She is associated with several powers including abilities to heal with cool water, induction of fertility and feminine essence, Women appeal to her for child-bearing and for the alleviation of female disorders. The Yoruba traditions described her as fond of babies and her intervention is sought if a baby becomes ill. Oshu in Yoruba traditions is also known for her love of honey.	circulatory system, digestive organs, elimination system, pubic area (female)
Shango	Associated with Virility, Masculinity, Fire, Lightning, Stones, Protector/Warrior, Magnetism. He is said to have abilities to transform base substance into that which is pure and valuable. He was the	reproductive system (male), bone marrow, life force or chi

	Oba of Oyo He derived his nickname Oba Koso from the annals of his immortality.		Yoruba beliefs she is the Orisha of rebirth as things must die so that new beginnings arise	
Oya	The other Wife of former Oba of Oyo called Shango (another Yoruba Orisha see above) said to turn into River Niger is often described as Tempest, Guardian of the Cemetery, Winds of Change, Storms, Progression, she is usually in the company of her husband Shango. In	lungs, bronchial passages, mucous membranes		

Titles and Processes

An "Onisegun" refers to a herbalist, Oloogun is one of several terms for a medical practitioner, and a Babalawo is a priest/priestess.

An "Oloogun", in addition to analyzing symptoms of the patient, look for the emotional and spiritual causes of the disease to placate the negative forces (ajogun) and only then will propose treatment that he/she deems appropriate. This may include herbs in the form of an infusion, enema, etc. In Yoruban medicine they also use dances, spiritual baths, symbolic sacrifice, song/prayer, and a change of diet to help cure the sick. They also believe that the only true and complete cure can be a change of "consciousness" where the individual can recognize the root of the problem themselves and seek to eliminate it. Disease to the Yorùbás is seen as a disruption of our connection with the Earth. "Physicians are often priests, priestesses, or high priests, or belong to a guild-like society hidden within tribal boundaries, completely secret to the outside world. In their communities, even obtaining an education in medicine may require becoming an initiate of one of these societies. The world view of a priest involves training and discipline to interpret events that are indicative of the nature of the patient's alignment internally with their own conscious and unrecognized issues, as well as with a variety of external forces and beings which inhabit our realm and require the inner vision and wisdom of the priest to interpret."

Yorubas are great believers of preventative medication. They are critical in the way they relate to modern western medicine. According to elite practitioners, if we listen to our bodies they will provide us with the preparation and appropriate knowledge we need to regain our balance with our immediate surroundings.

Source http://en.wikipedia.org/wiki/Yoruba_medicine

Yoruba music

The music of the Yoruba people of Nigeria and Benin are perhaps best known for an extremely advanced drumming tradition, especially using the dundun hourglass tension drums. Yoruba folk music became perhaps the most prominent kind of West African music in Afro-Latin and Caribbean musical styles. **Yorùbá music** left an especially important influence on the music used in Lukumi practice and the music of Cuba

Folk music

Ensembles using the dundun play a type of music that is also called *dundun*. These ensembles consist of various sizes of tension drums along with special band drums (*ogido*). The *gangan* is another such. The leader of a dundun ensemble is the *oniyalu* who uses the drum to "talk" by imitating the tonality

Omele ako, batá and two dunduns. Yoruba drummers in Kwara state.

of Yoruba. Much of Yoruba music is spiritual in nature, and this form is often devoted to Orisas.

Rhythmic structure

Iron agogô bells.

The most commonly used key pattern, or guide pattern in traditional Yoruba drumming is the seven-stroke figure known in ethnomusicology as the *standard pattern*. The standard pattern is expressed in both a triple-pulse (12/8 or 6/8) and a duple-pulse (4/4 or 2/2) structure. The standard pattern is often sounded on an iron bell.

Standard pattern in duple-pulse (4/4) and triple-pulse (12/8) form.

The strokes of the standard pattern coincide with: 1, 1a, 2& 2a, 3&, 4, 4a.
  12/8:

1 & a 2 & a 3 & a 4 & a ||
X . X . X X . X . X . X ||

4/4:

1 e & a 2 e & a 3 e & a 4 e & a ||
X . . X . X X . . X . X . . X ||

A great deal of Yoruba drum music is based in cross rhythm. The following example shows the five-stroke form of the standard pattern (known as clave in Afro-Latin music) on the kagano dundun drum (top line). The dunduns on the second and third lines sound an embellishment of the three-over-four (3:4) cross-rhythm—expressed as three pairs of strokes against four pairs of strokes.

Yoruba dundun ensemble.

Popular music

Yorùbá music is regarded as one of the more important components of the modern Nigerian popular music scene. Although traditional Yoruba music was not influenced by foreign music the same cannot be said of modern day Yoruba music which has evolved and adapted itself through contact with foreign instruments, talents and creativity. Interpretation involves rendering African, here Yoruba, musical expression using a mixture of instruments from different horizons.

Yoruba music traditionally centred around folklore and spiritual/deity worship, utilising basic and natural instruments such as clapping of the hands. Playing music for a living was not something the Yoruba's did and singers were referred to in a derogatory term of Alagbe, it is this derogation of musicians that made it not appeal to modern Yoruba at the time. Although, it is true that music genres like the highlife played by musicians like Rex Lawson, Segun Buckner, Bobby Benson, etc., Fela Kuti's Afrobeat and King Sunny Adé's juju are all Yoruba adaptations of foreign music. These musical genres have their roots in large metropolitan cities like Lagos, Ibadan, and Port Harcourt where people and culture mix influenced by their rich culture.

Some pioneering juju musicians include Tunde King, Tunde Nightingale, Why Worry in Ondo and Ayinde Bakare,Dele ojo, Ik Dairo Moses Olaiya (Baba Sala). sakara played by the pioneers such as Ojo Olawale in Ibadan, Abibu Oluwa, Yusuf Olatunji, Sanusi Aka, Saka Layigbade.

Apala, is another genre of Yoruba modern music which was played by spirited pacesetters such as Haruna Ishola, Sefiu Ayan, Ligali Mukaiba, Kasumu Adio, Yekini (Y.K.) Ajadi, etc.

Fuji, which emerged in the late 60s/early 70s, as an offshoot of were/ajisari music genres, which were made popular by certain Ibadan singers/musicians such as the late Sikiru Ayinde Barister, Alhaji Dauda Epo-Akara and Ganiyu Kuti or "Gani Irefin.

Another popular genre is waka music played and popularized by Alhaja Batuli Alake and, more recently, Salawa Abeni, Kuburat Alaragbo, Asanat Omo-Aje, Mujidat Ogunfalu, Misitura Atawe, Fatimo Akingbade, Karimot Aduke, and Risikat Abeawo. In both Ibadan (Nigeria's largest city), and Lagos (Nigeria's most populous city), these multicultural traditions were brought together and became the root of Nigerian popular music.

Musical instruments

Agbe: a shaker
Ashiko: a cone-shaped drum
Batá drum: a well decorated traditional drum of many tones, with strong links to the deity Shango, it produces sharp high tone sounds.
Goje: sort of violin like the sahelian **kora**
Sekere: a melodic shaker; beads or cowrie shells beautifully wound around a gourd, shaken, beaten by fists occasionally and thrown in the air to create a festive mood.
gudugudu: a smaller, melodic bata
Sakara drum: goatskin istretched over clay ring
Agogô: a high-pitched tone instrument like a "covered" 3-dimensional "tuning fork"
Saworo: like agogo, but its tone is low-pitched
aro: much like a saworo, low-pitched
Seli: a combination of aro, saworo and hand-clapping
Agidigbo, a thumb piano instrument wound round the neck and stabilized by the player's chest.
Dundun, consisting of *iya ilu* or *gbedu*, main or "mother" drum and omele, smaller drums, played as an accompaniment to bata drums to create a base for their sharp beats.
Bembé, bass drum, kettle drum. (see also List of Caribbean membranophones)
Source http://en.wikipedia.org/wiki/Yoruba_music

Yoruba name

Yoruba names are primarily used by the Yoruba people and Yoruba language-speaking individuals in both Nigeria and the Nigerian diaspora.

Naming ceremonies

By custom, Yoruba children are named in a ceremony that takes place 7 days after their birth. The names of the children are traditionally taken from the father, but names can also come from those of other ranking members of the family, including the mother, grandparents or next of kin. Both the mother and father and other next of kin can give their own favorite names to the child or children. Baby names often come from the grandparents and great grandparents of the child to be named.

Composition and importance of names

Yoruba names are often carefully considered during the week prior to the naming ceremony, as great care is placed upon selecting a name that would not reflect any sort of negativity or disrepute; in other words, selecting a name that previously belonged to a thief or criminal for a Yoruba child is not considered as a wise idea, as it (according to Yoruba philosophy) could result in the child growing up to become a thief or criminal.

Yoruba names are traditionally classified into two categories:
Destiny Names(Situational) also known as Oruko Amutorunwa ("names assumed to be brought from heaven" or derived from a religious background)
Acquired Names ("given on earth" or granted by next of kin)
One of the most common destiny names among the Yoruba are Taiwo (or Taiye) and Kehinde, which are given primarily to twins. And it is believed that the first of twin[s] is Taiwo (or Taiye), whose intention in coming out first is to perceives the kind of new environment they are before granting his/her second Kehinde (sometimes shortened to Kenny) to come out.

Acquired name may signify the position of the family in the society (e. g. "Adewale", a typical royal family name). It may also signify the family work (e.g. "Agbede", the blacksmith).

Yoruba also have "Oriki", a kind of praise recital used to emphasize the achievements of the ancestors of the family. Oriki could be a single word like "Adunni", or it could be a verse or a series of verses. Though not typically part of a standard name, the oriki is often used alongside one and is usually generally known to a person's contemporaries. Many an individual can even be recognised by the people of another town or even clan by using the oriki of his or her ancestral line.

Source http://en.wikipedia.org/wiki/Yoruba_name

Yoruba religion

The Yorùbá religion comprises the indigenous religion of the Yoruba people. Its homeland is in Southwestern Nigeria and the adjoining parts of Benin and Togo, a region that has come to be known as Yorubaland. Yorùbá religion is formed of diverse traditions and has no single founder. It has influenced or given birth to thriving ways of life such as Lucumí, Umbanda and Candomblé. Yoruba religious beliefs are part of itan, the total complex of songs, histories, stories and other cultural concepts which make up the Yorùbá society.

Beliefs

According to Kola Abimbola, the Yorùbá have evolved a robust philosophy. In brief, it holds that all human beings possess what is known as "Àyànmô" (destiny, fate) and are expected to eventually become one in spirit with Olódùmarè (Olòrún, the divine creator and source of all energy). Furthermore, the thoughts and actions of each person in Ayé (the physical realm) interact with all other living things, including the Earth itself.

Each person attempts to achieve transcendence and find their destiny in Òrún-Réré (the spiritual realm of those who do good and beneficial things). One's Orí-Inu (spiritual consciousness in the physical realm) must grow in order to consummate union with one's "Ipônri" (Orí Òrún, spiritual self).

Those who stop growing spiritually, in any of their given lives, are destined for "Òrún-Apadi" (Lit. the invisible realm of potsherds). Life and death are said to be cycles of existence in a series of physical bodies while one's spirit evolves toward transcendence. This evolution is said to be most evident amongst the Orishas, the divine viziers of the Almighty God.

Iwapęlę (or well-balanced) meditation and sincere veneration is sufficient to strengthen the Orí-Inu of most people. Well-balanced people, it is believed, are able to make positive use of the simplest form of connection between their Oris and the omnipotent Olu-Òrún: an adúra (petition or prayer) for divine support.

Prayer to one's Orí Òrún has been known to produce an immediate sensation of joy. Ęlégbara (Ęṣu, the divine messenger) initiates contact with Òrún on behalf of the petitioner, and transmits the prayer to Ayé; the deliverer of àṣę or *the spark of life*. He transmits this prayer without distorting it in any way. Thereafter, the petitioner may be satisfied with a personal answer. In the event that he or she is not, the Ifa oracle of the Orisha Orunmila may also be consulted. All communication with Òrún, whether simplistic in the form of a personal prayer or complicated in the form of that done by an initiated priest of divination, however, is energized by invoking àṣę.

In the Yorùbá belief system, Olódùmarè has àṣę over all that is. It is for this reason that He is considered supreme.

According to one of the Yorùbá accounts of creation, during a certain stage in this process, the "truth" was sent to confirm the habitability of the newly formed planets. The earth being one of these was visited but deemed too wet for conventional life.

After a successful period of time, a number of divinities were commanded to accomplish the task of helping earth develop its crust. On one of their visits to the realm, the arch-divinity Obatala took to the stage equipped with a mollusk that held in its shell some form of soil; two winged beasts and some cloth like material. He emptied the soil onto what soon became a large mound on the surface of the water and soon after, the winged-beasts began to scatter this around until the point where it gradually made into a large patch of dry land; the various indentations they created eventually becoming hills and valleys.

Obatala leaped on to a high-ground and named the place Ife. The land became fertile and plant life began to flourish. From handfuls of earth he began to mould figurines. Meanwhile, as this was happening on earth, Olódùmarè gathered the gasses from the far reaches of space and sparked an explosion that shaped into a fireball. He subsequently sent it to Ife, where it dried much of the land and simultaneously began to bake the motionless figurines. It was at this point that Olódùmarè released the "breath of life" to blow across the land, and the figurines slowly came into "being" as the first people of Ife.

For this reason, Ile-Ife is locally referred to as the "cradle of existence".

Olódùmarè

Olódùmarè is the most important "state of existence". Regarded as being all-encompassing, no gender can therefore be assigned. Hence, it is common to hear references to "it" or "they" (although this is meant to address a somewhat singularity) in usual speech. "They" are the owner of all heads, for during human creation, Olódùmarè gave "êmí" (the breath of life) to humankind. In this, Olódùmarè is Supreme

Perhaps one of the most important human endeavors extolled within the tribe's literary corpus is the quest to better one's "Iwa" (character, behaviour). In this way the teachings transcends religious doctrine, advising as it does that a person must also better his civic, social and intellectual spheres of being; every stanza of the sacred Ifa oracular poetry has a portion covering the importance of "Iwa". Central to this is the theme of righteousness, both individual and collective.

An Alternative Version Of The Creation

The Yorùbá regard Olódùmarè as the principal agent of creation.

In another telling of the creation myth, Olódùmarè (also called Olorun) is the creator. In the beginning there is only water. Olódùmarè sends Obatala to bring forth land. Obatala descended from above on a long chain, bringing with him a rooster, some earth, and some iron. He stacked the iron in the water, the earth on the iron, and the chicken atop the earth. The chicken kicked and scattered the earth, creating land. Some of the other divinities descended upon it to live with Obatala. One of them, Chameleon, came first to judge if the earth was dry. When he said that it was, Olódùmarè called the land *Ife* for "wide". Obatala then created humans out of earth and called Olódùmarè to blow life into them. Some say Obatala was jealous and wished to be the only giver of life, but Olódùmarè put him to sleep as he worked. Conversely, it is also said by others that it is Obatala who shapes life while it is still in the womb.

Divinities

An Orisha (Orisa or Orixa) is an entity that possesses the capability of reflecting some of the manifestations of Olódùmarè. Yòrùbá *Orishas* (translated "owners of heads") are often described as intermediaries between man and the supernatural. The term is often translated as "deities" or "divinities".

Orisha(s) are more like "anamistic entities" and have control over specific elements in nature, thus being better referred to as the divinities. Even so, there are those of their number that are more akin to ancient heroes and/or sages. These are best addressed as dema deities. Even though in the basics of things, the term Orisha is often used to acknowledge a many divine entities, is mainly reserved for the former.

Orishas	Attributes
Orunmila	The Yorùbá Grand Priest and custodian of the Ifa Oracle, source of knowledge who is believed to oversee the knowledge of the Human Form, Purity, the Cures of illnesses and deformities. His subordinate priests or followers are the Awos.
Èṣù or Elegbara	Often ill-translated as "The Devil" or "The Evil Being", Èṣù is in truth neither of these. Best referred to as "The Trickster", he deals a hand of misfortune to those that do not offer tribute or are deemed to be *spiritual novices*. Also regarded as the "divine messenger", a prime negotiator between negative and positive forces in the body and an enforcer of the "law of being". He is said to assist in enhancing the power derived from herbal medicines. Eshu is the orisha of chance, accident and unpredictability. Because he is Olorun's linguist and the master of languages, Eshu is responsible for carrying messages and sacrifices from humans to the Sky God. Also known for his phallic powers and exploits. Eshu is said to lurk at gateways, on the highways and at the crossroads, where he introduces chance and accident into the lives of humans. Known by a variety of names, including Elegbara.
Ogun	The divinity of iron and metallurgy.
Yemoja	Mother of Waters, Nurturer of Water Resources. According to Olorishas, she is the amniotic fluid in the womb of the pregnant woman, as well as the breasts which nurture. She is considered the protective energy of the feminine force.

Oshun	Wife of the former Oba of Oyo called Shango (another Yoruba Orisha, see below) is said to've turned into a river in Osogbo. The Yoruba clerics ascribed to her Sensuality, Beauty and Gracefulness, symbolizing both their people's search for clarity and a flowing motion. She is associated with several powers, including abilities to heal with cool water, induction of fertility and the control of the feminine essence. Women appeal to her for child-bearing and for the alleviation of female disorders. The Yoruba traditions describe her as being fond of babies and her intervention is sought if a baby becomes ill. Oshun is also known for her love of honey.
Shango	Associated with Virility, Masculinity, Fire, Lightning, Stones, Warriors and Magnetism. He is said to have the abilities to transform base substances into those that are pure and valuable. He was the Oba of Oyo at some point in its history. He derived his nickname Oba Koso from the tales of his immortality. Shango is the orisha of the thunderbolt, said to have ruled in ancient times over the kingdom of Oyo. Also known as Jakuta (Stone Thrower) and as Oba Koso (The King Does Not Hang).
Oya	The other wife of the former Oba of Oyo called Shango (another Yoruba Orisha, see above), she is said to've turned into the River Niger. She is often described as the Tempest, Guardian of the Cemetery, Winds of Change, Storms and Progression. Due to her personal power, she is usually depicted as being in the company of her husband Shango. Orisha of rebirth.

Irúnmôlè

Irúnmôlè are entities sent by the Supreme (Olódùmarè) to complete given tasks, often acting as liaisons between Orun (the invisible realm) and Aiye (the physical realm). Irúnmôlè(s) can best be described as ranking divinities; whereby such divinities are regarded as the principal Orishas.

Reincarnation

A Egungun masquerade dance garment in the permanent collection of The Children's Museum of Indianapolis

The Yoruba believe in reincarnation within the family. The names Babatunde (father returns), Yetunde (Mother returns), Babatunji (Father wakes once again) and Sotunde (The wise man returns) all offer vivid evidence of the Ifa concept of familial or lineal rebirth. There is no simple guarantee that your grandfather or great uncle will "come back" in the birth of your child, however.

Whenever the time arrives for a spirit to return to Earth (otherwise known as The Marketplace) through the conception of a new life in the direct bloodline of the family, one of the component entities of a person's being returns, while the other remains in Heaven (Ikole Orun). The spirit that returns does so in the form of a Guardian Ori. One's Guardian Ori, which is represented and contained in the crown of the head, represents not only the spirit and energy of one's previous blood relative, but the accumulated wisdom he or she has acquired through a myriad of lifetimes. This is not to be confused with one's spiritual Ori, which contains personal destiny, but instead refers to the coming back to *The Marketplace* of one's personal blood Ori through one's new life and experiences. The Primary Ancestor (which should be identified in your Itefa) becomes - if you are aware and work with that specific energy - a "guide" for the individual throughout their lifetime. At the end of that life they return to their identical spirit self and merge into one, taking the additional knowledge gained from their experience with the individual as a form of *payment*.

Yoruba religion around the world

According to Professor S. A. Akintoye, the Yorùbá are/were exquisite statesmen spread across the globe in an unprecedented fashion; the reach of their culture is largely due to migration of personnel. Some of this movement occurred during periods that pre-date the Egyptian dynasties; whilst the most recent migration occurred during the "holocaust" (i.e. The Trans-Atlantic Slave Trade) of the 1300–1900. During this period of holocaust, many were captured and sold into the Atlantic slave trade and transported to Cuba, the Dominican Republic, Puerto Rico, Brazil, Venezuela and other parts of the World. With them, they carried their religious beliefs. The school-of-thought integrated into what now constitutes the core of the "New World lineages":
Santería or "regla lucumi" (Cuba)
Oyotunji (U.S.)
Candomblé (Brazil)
Umbanda (Brazil)
Batuque (Brazil)

Relationship with Vodou

The popularly known Vodou faith, said to have originated amongst a different ethnic group (the Gba speaking peoples of modern Benin, Togo and Ghana), shares some similarities with the religion, and may even be taken to be theologically related on a superficial level.

Source http://en.wikipedia.org/wiki/Yoruba_religion

Yoruba traditional art

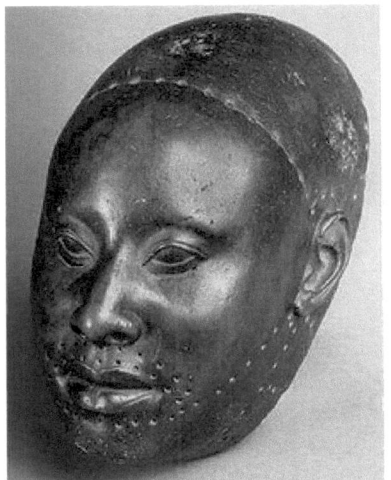

Yoruba bronze head sculpture, Ife, Nigeria c. 12th century A.D.

The Yoruba of South Western Africa (Benin Republic, Nigeria and Togo, also including parts of Ghana, Cameroon and Sierra Leone), have a very rich and vibrant artisan community, creating traditional and contemporary art. The custom of art and artisans among the Yoruba is deeply rooted in the Ifá literary corpus, indicating the orishas Ogun, Obatala, Oshun and Obalufon as central to creation mythology including artistry (i.e. the art of humanity).

Over the years, many have come to merge foreign ideas of artistry and contemporary art with the traditional art forms found in West Africa. The traditional art forms among the Yoruba include but are not limited to: beading, braiding, tattooing, clay moulding and ceramic work, bronze casting, weaving and dyeing, sculpting, etc.

There is also a vibrant form of customary theatre known as *Alarinjo* that has its roots in the medieval period and that has given much to the contemporary Nigerian film industry.

Metal arts

Yoruban blacksmiths create sculpture from iron, through hand-beating, welding, and casting. Ogun is honored as the god of iron.

Metalworkers also create brass sculptures by lost-wax casting. Brass is seen as being incorruptible by the Ogboni Society.

Ife head, terracotta, probably 12–14th centuries

Another head from Ife from about the same time.

Sculpure of a 'Queen Mother' from Benin.

16th century ivory mask from Benin

One of the Benin Bronzes, 16th-18th century, Nigeria.

Source http://en.wikipedia.org/wiki/Yoruba_traditional_art

Article summaries

The meaning of home in Yoruba culture

Author: Y Okeyinka; B Amole
Description: This study examined the meaning of home in Yoruba culture in Ogbomoso Nigeria Africa. Ogbomoso is one of Yoruba cities that reveals the innate social and cultural tendencies of traditional Yoruba cities. Data for the studies were collected from residents of houses categorised into five types of family house, single family dwelling, apartment, duplex and rooming houses Purposive sampling technique was utilised to obtain information from head of these houses. Subjecting the data collected from residents toanalysis, the study provided information that 40.3 %, 22.8%, 17.3%, 12.5% and 5.3% choose the single family dwelling, duplex, apartment, family house, rooming house or "face me i face you" in descendingorder as the house that respondent readily think of as home, Furthermore the result of a factor analysis also provided information that 16.95%, 8.33% and 7.13% of variances refers to availability of functional spaces, emotional factor and privacy respectively out of nine factors which define the meaning of home in Ogbomosho. Data was also collected using an in-depth interview, the result of the analysis provided information that the home means the cradle, a place of comfort, shelter, a place of abode and safety, and a house with facilities that gives comfortable living. The study found that there is significant relationship between private nature of conveniences in houses which directly influence comfort and privacy and this could explain why the single family dwelling, duplex and apartment were rated as homes to the respondent. Generally home means a shelter and a place of abode, a single family dwelling. This is because premium is set on ownership of a house in Yoruba culture. This meaning of home as the cradle and source of origin is supported by the general cultural belief of the Yoruba.Key words: Meaning, House, Home, Yoruba culture, Cradle, Premium
Publisher: Ethiopian Journal of Environmental Studies and Management
Year of Publication: 2012-10-18
URL: http://www.ajol.info/index.php/ejesm/article/view/82354

TOWARDS A RECONSTRUCTION OF YORUBA CULTURE

Author: ALERU, Jonathan Olu; ALABI, Raphael Ajayi
Description: This paper discusses the signifi cance of toponymy in historical and archaeological reconstructions especially as it relates to the culture history of Yorubaland. Drawing case studies from two extreme areas of the region; Igbominaland and Badagry coastal area, it is observed that toponymy provides useful information which is relevant as sources for many aspects of the culture history and archaeology of the region. It is concluded that, even though the hints provided by toponymy are of very high reliability, they however need to be corroborated by oral, historical, and archaeological sources.
Publisher: The Center for African Area Studies, Kyoto University
Year of Publication: 2010-12
URL: http://hdl.handle.net/2433/139278

Art and the Perception of Women in Yorùbá Culture

Author: Henry Drewal
Description: H. Drewal — ~L'art et le concept de féminité dans la culture yoruba.~ La conception de l'essence féminine chez les Yoruba est dominée par la notion d'intériorité (ori inûn), à laquelle se rattachent les notions de secret, de calme, de froid et la couleur blanche, qui s'opposent terme à terme aux notions symétriques caractérisant la masculinité. Les femmes ménopausées (et, dans une moindre mesure, impubères, enceintes ou allaitant) sont chargées d'une force magique, ~àṣe~, supérieure à celle des ~òrìṣà.~ Ces caractéristiques et ces pouvoirs sont symbolisés dans le masque barbu et voilé de blanc de la Grande Mère, Ìyánlá, personnage central du culte Èfè-Gèlèdé, à la fois secret et accessible aux membres de la communauté.
Publisher: PERSEE
Year of Publication: 1977
URL: http://www.persee.fr/web/revues/home/prescript/article/cea_0008-0055_1977_num_17_68_2430

Yoruba Culture and Its Influence on The Development of Modern Popular Music in Nigeria

Author: Adedeji, Adewale
Description: This thesis focuses on the contributions of the Yorùbá culture to the development of modern Nigerian popular music. It traces the origin, conception and growth of popular music styles in Nigeria and highlights the underlying Yorùbá cultural cum linguistic influence that nurtured their growth within the urban space of Lagos city. It examines how contemporary Nigerian popular music practitioners appropriate the Yorùbá culture in negotiating their musical and national identities and counteract popular music homogenization through the creation of hybrid musical styles and cultures. The work adopts a multi-dimensional research approach that involves cultural, musicological, historical, anthropological and socio-linguistical tools. Adopting the participant-observer method with Lagos as the primary fieldwork site, additional data were sourced along with interviews of key informants through bibliographic and discographic methods. The study reveals the importance of Lagos as a major factor that contributed to the development of Nigeria's popular music practice as exemplified in genres like jùjú, fújì and afrobeat, and discovers that the Yorùbá language has gradually become the dominant medium through which artists express their musical identity as typified by current mainstream hip hop music. Extending earlier work by scholars such as Barber, Waterman

and Euba and recent works in hip hop linguistics by Alim and Omoniyi, the thesis contributes to the growing body of research within popular music through the discipline of ethnomusicology, especially in the emerging area of academic inquiry into indigenous African hip hop culture.
Publisher: University of Sheffield
Year of Publication: 2010-12-17
URL: http://etheses.whiterose.ac.uk/2257/

The Interaction of Prophecy and Yoruba Culture in Selected African Indigenous Churches

Author: Adekunle Oyinloye Dada; University of Ibadan, Nigeria
Description: Prophecy and prophetism are important elements of liturgical activities in the African indigenous churches in Nigeria. For the adherents of these churches, prophecy has not ceased in that God still communicates with them. This background therefore justifies the emphasis placed on prophetic activities in the indigenous churches in Nigeria. The goal of this paper is to critically examine the influence of the traditional Yoruba culture and religion in the expression of prophetic phenomena and on prophetic personages in these churches. As corollary the paper will also explore how these churches' concept of prophetic inspiration, call, and the inducement of the psychic states have been shaped by the Yoruba religio-cultural milieu.
Publisher: Equinox Publishing Ltd
Year of Publication: 2009-06-12
URL: http://www.equinoxpub.com/index.php/BT/article/view/5613

The Vestige Of Court Poetry In Modern Yoruba Music: A Study Of Sikiru Ayinde Barrister

Author: B Mekus
Description: This article examines the retention of some features of traditional court poetry in modern Yoruba music. The article's focus is the juju music even as Sikiru Ayinde Barrister attracts the attention of the article. Efforts are made to establish the similarities between court poets and modern musicians in the performance of the roles of checks and balances, drawing from the memories of the past, both good and bad in order to propel towards a glorious tomorrow. Characteristic of the traditional court poets, modern musicians explore, to the maximum, the unique privilege of remarking on the king/leader and his activities for his good and that of the people he presides over. Therefore, leisure, sought in music, provides education, sensibility, training, construction and reconstruction to ensure: a better living, a wonderful co-existence and, possibly an articulate global community. Keywords: Court poetry, Yoruba music, juju music.Indilinga Vol. 7 (1) 2008: pp. 23-36
Publisher: Indilinga: African Journal of Indigenous Knowledge Systems
Year of Publication: 2008-10-09
URL: http://ajol.info/index.php/indilinga/article/view/26390

A Lexico-syntactic Comparative Analysis of Ondo and Ikale Dialects of the Yoruba Language

Author: Ayeomoni, Omoniyi Moses; Obafemi Awolowo University
Description: The study was a comparative study of Ondo and Ikale dialects of the Yoruba language with a view to finding out the areas of convergences and divergences between the two dialects. The study was based on 50 sentences selected from each of the dialects, but only 25 of the sentences were presented and used in this study. They were anaylsed from the perspective of Halliday Systemic Function Grammar (SFG) in order to identify the prominent lexemes and syntactic structures in the two dialects. Simple statistics based on percentages was used to calculate the number of lexemes and structures that are similar and different. It was discovered that the two dialects have basically the same lexemes at both subject and predicator levels This shows that the speakers of the two dialects often make use of the same nominal and verbal items in their speeches. Besides, the two dialects share basically the same syntactic components – Subjects, Predicator, Complement and Adjunct as found in all the sentences examined. The dialects are however, found to be mainly different in the area of auxiliary verbs. Most of the words or lexemes in the dialects are also found in the standard Yoruba language, hence the mutual intelligibility of the two dialects to an average Yoruba language native speaker. It is thus envisaged that other dialects of Yoruba language that are geographically close may equally share similar linguistic features in the areas of lexemes and syntax.
Publisher: ACADEMY PUBLISHER
Year of Publication: 2012-09-01
URL: http://ojs.academypublisher.com/index.php/tpls/article/view/tpls020918021810

A DENTAL HEALTH EDUCATION VIDEO FOR NIGERIAN CHILDREN IN THE YORUBA LANGUAGE

Author: Olubunmi Olusola Bankole; University of Ibadan
Description: Abstract The development of this video titled "Itoju Eyin" (meaning care of the teeth) was prompted by the fact that research findings revealed poor oral hygiene among Nigerian children from the lower socioeconomic class. Videos have been employed as a medium of dental health education and research has shown them to be useful and valuable visual aids . This may be attributed to the fact that what is seen is usually retained better having a lasting impression on the target population The video was produced in the Yoruba language which serves as a culturally appropriate dental health education tool for children particularly in south western Nigeria . The video particularly targets children from the lower socioeconomic class.
Publisher: University of Ibadan
Year of Publication: 2011-07-03
URL: http://www.ajbrui.net/ojs/index.php/ajbr/article/view/117

These are less relevant articles. To read a complete article simply search the title at Google, Bing or your local library's web site:

Barry Hallen, The Good, the

Bad, and the Beautiful: Discourse about Values in Yoruba Culture. (Book Review)

© Africa March 22, 2003

BARRY HALLEN, The Good, the Bad, and the Beautiful: Discourse about Values in Yoruba Culture. Bloomington IN: Indiana University Press, 2001, 256 pp., US39.95, ISBN 0 253 33806 9 hard covers, US$17.95 (12.95 [pounds sterling]), 0 253 21416 5 paperback.

Knowing about knowing marks the philosophical sub-field of epistemology. This is the starting point of Barry Hallen's new book, the central assumption being that, in Yoruba discourse, 'the epistemic becomes a kind of master key, a passe partout, to the value system' (p. 65). This provides the starting point and overall structure of his book. Culturally specific epistemological frameworks, Hallen argues, are the basis of normative discourse on morality and aesthetics, two further sub-fields of philosophy. Hallen shows us why and how this is so for the Yoruba context from the perspective of ordinary language philosophy. In doing so he expands his long-standing contribution to the development of an analytical school within African philosophy.

The Good, the Bad, and the Beautiful is a sequel to Knowledge, Belief and Witchcraft, co-authored with J. O. Sodipo and recently reprinted in an expanded edition. Here the 'analytic experiments in African philosophy', as ...

Rhythms of the gods: music and spirituality in Yoruba culture.

© Journal of Pan African Studies March 1, 2010

Introduction: Asa and Esin in Yoruba Performance

The constant engagement between the elements of play and spirituality in Yoruba performance provides the setting for understanding the role of the Yoruba performer as a mediator between temporal and spiritual domains of existence.

Yoruba masquerade performances are particularly illustrative of such mediatory roles. The masker, usually a male, physically relates to the human audiences who follow, tease, praise, observe, and perform with him. He must also relate to the divine presence of the ancestral forces that he embodies. The masker, just like the drummer, or the singer, performs within religious rituals, thereby navigating a balance between the two different modes of experience that he connects. For while, on the one hand, he must deal with esoteric narratives and age-long rituals that communicate directly with deities, he must, on the other hand, also respond and relate to the social situations within which religious rituals derive meaning in real life terms.

As liminal agents inhabiting the threshold of these two spaces, the Yoruba performer connects the living with the spiritual; life with death; body with soul; as well as the aesthetic with the divine. Commenting on the ...

Rhythms of the Gods: Music, Spirituality and Social Engagement in Yoruba Culture

© The Journal of Pan African Studies (Online) June 1, 2010

Abstract

The notions of "icons as objects" and "icons as act" (Kasfir, 1998: 20) are used to analyze the mediatory role of Yorùbá musicians in meeting the spiritual and the social needs of their communities. The author explains that Yoruba performers are constantly aware of the discursive engagement between àsà (social engagement and cultural practice) and èsìn (spiritual devotion), and posits that there is a conceptual engagement between the mediating role of Yoruba performers and the thematic and structural features of their performances. This fact speaks to the constant interaction between play and spirituality as controlled by the agency of the performer, and draws attention ...

The Good, the Bad, and the Beautiful: Discourse about Values in Yoruba Culture/A Short History of African Philosophy

© African Studies Review September 1, 2003

SCIENCE AND PHILOSOPHY Barry Hallen. The Good, the Bad, and the Beautiful: Discourse about Values in Yoruba Culture. Bloomington: Indiana University Press, 20001. xiv + 219 pp. Notes. Bibliography. Index. $39.95. Cloth. $17.95. Paper.

Barry Hallen. A Short History of African Philosophy. Bloomington: Indiana University Press, 2002. ix + 130 pp. Bibliography. $29.95. Cloth. $14. 95. Paper.

"What is important in a study such as this is to be careful-to try not to misrepresent Afican meanings and attitudes" (9). The emphasis is Hallen's, yet it appears to be shared by all the participants in his project. Hallen's own presence in the opening chapter of The Good, the Bad, and the ...

The Good, the Bad, and the Beautiful: Discourse about Values in Yoruba Culture.(Book Review)

© African Arts September 22, 2002

Barry Hallen

Indiana University Press, Bloomington and Indianapolis, 2000. 201 pp., appendix, glossary, bibliography, index. $39.95 hardcover, $17.95 softcover.

It's no secret that most of the Western world persists in regarding "African thought" as an oxymoron. The old misperceptions die hard in the popular imagination, and also, it seems, in certain quarters of the academy. Readers of African Arts already know the litany of arbitrary oppositions, traceable back to the philosopher G.W.F. Hegel (1837) and beyond: Africans live in timeless intimacy with forces of spirit and myth rather than in the historical time of scientific Progress. As passive followers of cultural "traditions" rather than as intrepid innovators, they exist not as individuals but as "tribes." Thinking through pre-given affective symbols instead of empirically based reason, they have customs rather than laws, beliefs rather than knowledge. And of course, they create "fetishes," not "art." No need to continue this list of faulty assumptions--which have been well criticized in the pages of this very journal, among many others.

Barry Hallen is a philosopher who, like many working today in the fields of African culture studies, is ...

Yoruba Religion

© Encyclopedia of Religion January 1, 2005

YORUBA RELIGION . The twelve to fifteen million Yoruba people of southwestern Nigeria, the Republic of Benin (formerly Dahomey), and Togo (topographically the area is defined as that between 6°0–9°5' 2°41'–6° east longitude) are the heirs of one of the oldest cultural traditions in West Africa. Archaeological and linguistic evidence indicate that the Yoruba have lived in their present habitat since at least the fifth century bce. The development of the regional dialects that distinguish the Yoruba subgroups and the process of urbanization, which developed into a social system unique among sub-Saharan African peoples, took place during the first millennium bce. By the ninth century the ancient city of Ile-Ifẹ was thriving, and in the next five centuries Ifẹ artists would create terracotta and bronze sculptures that are now among Africa's artistic treasures.

Both Yoruba myth and oral history refer to Oduduwa (also known as Odua) as the first king and founder of the Yoruba people. Some myths portray him as the creator god and assert that the place of creation was Ile-Ifẹ, which subsequently became the site of Oduduwa's throne. Oral history, however, suggests that the story of Oduduwa's assumption of the throne at Ifẹ refers to a conquest of the ...

DIVERSITY WITHIN YORUBA-LANGUAGE VIDEO FILMS

© African Studies Review September 1, 2012

Olu Olowogemo. Bosun Omo Yankee. 2011. Nigeria. Yoruba, with English subtitles. Nigeria. High-Waves Video Mart. 275 min. No price reported.

Funke Akindele and Abbey Lanre. Omo Getto. 2011. Nigeria. Yoruba, with English subtitles. Olasco Films Nigeria Ltd. 174 min. No price reported.

Tunde Kelani. Ma'ami. 2011. Nigeria. English, Yoruba, with English subtitles. Mainframe Productions. 92 min. No price reported.

After two decades of prolific growth, Nigeria's video film industry, commonly called Nollywood, has garnered significant scholarly attention. The emergence of Nollywood studies is indebted to several seminal surveys, including Jonathan Haynes and Onokome ...

Sex and the Empire That is no More: Gender and the Politics of Metaphor in Oyo Yoruba Religion. (reprint, 1994). (RELIGION)(Brief Article)(Book Review)

© Reference & Research Book News August 1, 2005
BL2480
2004-046221
1-57181-307-1

Sex and the empire that is no more; gender and the politics of metaphor in Oyo Yoruba religion. (reprint, 1994)
Matory, J. Lorand.
Berghahn Books, [c]2005
295 p.
$25.00 (pa)

In the 1994 U. of Minnesota Press edition, Matory (anthropology, African and African American studies, Harvard U.) proposed a 'new politics of ...

Sex and the Empire That Is No More: Gender and the Politics of Metaphor in Oyo Yoruba Religion

© The International Journal of African Historical Studies May 1, 2006

Sex and the Empire That Is No More: Gender and the Politics of Metaphor in Oyo Yoruba Religion. By J. Lorand Matory. second edition. New York and Oxford: Berghahn Books, 2005. Pp. xlii, 295; 18 figures. $25.95 / £17.00 paper.

This second edition of the seminal Sex and the Empire That Is No More by J. Lorand Matory seems more salient in retrospect as the international interest in orisha worship and the meaning of transatlantic aesthetics that claim a Yoruba ancestry increases. This new edition is situated nicely by Matory in a preface that accounts for reactions to the initial study, particularly by Oyeronke Oyewumi in terms of "Yoruba" approaches to gender and society. To ...

Yoruba Religion and Culture in the Americas

© Encyclopedia of African-American Culture and History January 1, 2006

The Yoruba presence in the Americas is evident in Cuban Santería, Brazilian Candomblé and Xangô, and the Orisha and Shango religions of Trinidad and Grenada. Less well known are the St. Lucian Kele, or Shango cult, and Jamaican Kumina. These diasporic religions are testimony to the memory and determination of those Africans and their descendants who retained their sacred traditions, often in the face of attempts to marginalize or eliminate them. Some returned to Africa to renew their knowledge. Brazilian Candomblé has been nourished by ongoing contact with its sources of origin. In recent years, Nigerian traditional religious leaders have visited Cuba, Brazil, and Trinidad.

Many features of diasporic Orisha worship remain close to their origins, including myths, elements of ritual, language, material culture, and the names of deities. Yet changes have also occurred. These reflect the challenges of transmission, societal constraints on practice, and encounters with other cultures. Today, people of all colors can assume a Yoruba identity through initiation into the religion. Religious teachings formerly handed down solely by word of mouth are now available in written form. Equivalents for the plants and herbs used for healing ...

Sex and the Empire That Is No More: Gender and the Politics of Metaphor in Oyo Yoruba Religion.

© Journal of the Royal Anthropological Institute June 1, 1997

This is an innovative ritual history of the Rendering of power relations in the former Oyo Empire and its current practices in the possession cults in Igboho, an Oyo North town in Nigeria where the author did fieldwork during the 1980s.

Matory introduces this study with the hypothesis that the Oyo Yoruba do not conceptualize gender differentiation and hierarchy in terms of men's or women's achievements nor in terms of the biological difference between the sexes. Gender bending in ritual and kinship terminology is pervasive, but the hub of his argument centres on the possession cults of some of the most popular pan-Yoruba orisha (deities). Historically; these cults are closely associated with the former Oyo empire, and their most important deity is the thunder god Shango, the mythical ancestor of the Alafin, Oyo's sacred king. The river goddess Yemoia is Shango's mother, …

Yoruba Creativity: Fiction, Language, Life and Songs

© The International Journal of African Historical Studies January 1, 2006
Yoruba Creativity: Fiction, Language, Life and Songs. Edited by Toyin Falola and Ann Geneva. Trenton, N.J.: African World Press, 2005. Pp. viii, 350; 7 illustrations, 22 figures, 3 tables; index. $109.95 cloth, $34.95 paper.

This edited volume grew out of the international conference, "Perspectives on Yoruba History and Culture," held at the University of Texas-Austin in March 2004, attended by scholars from throughout the Yoruba Diaspora. Conference participants focused on aspects of Yoruba language-both written and oral-that are reflected in the four sections of the subsequent book: Fiction, Life and Drama, Language, and Songs. In the book's introduction, the co-editors frame …

Yoruba

© Worldmark Encyclopedia of Cultures and Daily Life January 1, 2009
PRONUNCIATION: YAWR-uh-buh
LOCATION: West Africa (primarily Nigeria; also Benin and Togo)
POPULATION: 19,327,000
LANGUAGE: Yoruba
RELIGION: Ancestral religion, Islam, Christianity
RELATED ARTICLES: Vol. 1: Beninese; Nigerians

INTRODUCTION

The Yoruba are one of the largest and most important ethnic groups south of the Sahara desert. Their tradition of urban life is unique among African ethnic groups. The Yoruba rank among the leaders in economics, government, religion, and artistic achievement in West Africa. Within Nigeria, where they dominate the Western part of the country, the Yoruba are one of the three largest and most important ethnic groups. The Yoruba people are not a single group, but are a series of diverse people bound together by common language, dress, ritual, political system, mythology, and history.

There has been much speculation about the origins of the Yoruba people. Based on their beautifully cast brass sculptures from Ife, one opinion held that Yoruba culture had been introduced by Etruscans who reached West Africa by way of the "lost continent" of Atlantis. Others suggested that the Yoruba may have come from Egypt. Many educated Yoruba people accept this view, which is also supported by theories relating to similarities …

Not just music: rhythm, language and poetry.(Book review)

© African Business December 1, 2007
Routes to Roots
Yoruba Drums from Nigeria
By Sola Akingbola
Arc Music
Cat: EUCD2114
With this CD, Sola Akingbola, the long-standing percussionist with the international, chart-topping band Jamiroquai, presents a superb album of Yoruba percussion from Nigeria. He finds his way back to his roots exploring the unique melodies, rhythmic structures and philosophical poetry of the Yoruba people.

Akingbola has spent most of his life in London, UK, but his roots are in Oregun, Nigeria, where he was born to Yoruba parents. Describing his relationship to Nigeria as a musical, this album reveals his passion for the language of …

II 'Cultural officer' at home and abroad: Oloye Adebayo Ogunrinu Ogundijo, 1939-2005. (AFRICAN MEMOIRS)(Biography)

© Africa January 1, 2010
ON THE CAREER OF A CHRISTIAN SCHOOL TEACHER TURNED ORISA PRIEST

His friends addressed him as Oloye (Titleholder) and as Bayo. He was deeply rooted in the world-views, folk classifications of living beings, healing practices and social mores of modern urban forms of Yoruba culture. These are of course widespread cultural forms, which constantly cut across the hypothetical divide between what counts as 'popular culture' and what is classified as 'elite culture' or 'academic culture' in contemporary Yorubaland. They, and the social-networking practices and hierarchical conventions accompanying them, largely shaped Bayo's assumptions and attitudes throughout his life. At the same time, as his career demonstrates, he was a man of initiative and insight, quick to detect new paths and eager to take them.

For many years, at Obafemi Awolowo University, Ile-Ife, he held the position of cultural officer in the Institute of Cultural Studies, where the 'academic' and 'popular', and the 'modern' and 'traditional' dimensions of Yoruba culture intersect. In Nigeria he published books in Yoruba and English, which are compromises between different orders of conventions in the presentation of the material. (1) Also, as a deservedly …

Santería Aesthetics

© Encyclopedia of African-American Culture and History January 1, 2006
Santería aesthetics is a Yoruba-American artistic expression rooted in the history of enslaved Africans' desire to preserve their religion and culture during their enslavement in the Americas. Art is seminal to the cultural identity of all

African peoples and, in particular, the Yoruba of southwestern Nigeria, for whom the arts are intricately connected to their religion. Yoruba artistic preeminence in the visual arts is legendary, dating back to the first millennium. In *Flash of the Spirit*, African art historian Robert Farris Thompson (1983) stated, "Yoruba assess everything aesthetically." Thompson's observation applies to the Yoruba diaspora as well. Everywhere in the Americas where the Yoruba presence is found there is evidence that art and aesthetics play a dominant role in daily life. According to Yoruba religious belief, Olodumare, the supreme being, sent down lesser deities known as *orishas* to begin life on earth. One of the first *orishas* sent by Olodumare was Obatalá, who was given charge of creativity.

The transatlantic slave trade brought about the dispersal of Yoruba religion and culture in the Americas, particularly in Cuba, Brazil, Haiti, and Trinidad, where the first wave of the Yoruba diaspora landed. With the ...

Afro-Brazilians in Salvador: reflections of a West African Christian. (Conference on World Mission and Evangelism)(Mission in the Twenty-First Century: Impulses from Salvador)

© International Review of Mission January 1, 1997

The writer in Brazil: reflections on the distant past and recent past

I lived in Brazil for two years during the past decade. My base was Rio de Janeiro. Before moving there I spent time preparing for my encounter with an entirely different culture. Part of my study included reading materials on the religions of this country So, during the first weekend of my stay evidence of African Tradition Religion (ATR) was seen in the form of sacrifices (decapitated chickens in a bucket) and symbols of peace (red roses) on the street comers. I knew then that the resources read in preparation for the journey were not just propaganda.

During that period, the Protestant churches in Rio de Janeiro had little tolerance for persons who practised ATRs. The main emphasis was on rebuke, condemnation and isolation. The evangelists' approach to these persons was all or nothing. One must become a Christian by standards outside his or her culture. Even in the twentieth century the vestiges of Portugal and Spain's idea of Christendom left its mark on the church in Brazil. Yet devotees of the other ...

...

Women in the Yoruba Religious Sphere

© African Studies Review December 1, 2006

WOMEN & GENDER Oyeronke Olajubu. Women in the Yoruba Religious Sphere. Albany: State University of New York Press, 2003. Bibliography. Index. $49.50. Cloth. $16.95. Paper.

This work is an exploration of the interplay of gender and power relations in the worlds of Yoruba religion. Contrary to the general assumption that women play only limited roles in Yoruba religious traditions, Olajubu argues that as the principal repositories of these traditions, Yoruba women are crucial to the conceptualization and practice of both indigenous religion and Christianity. Based on an array of oral and written sources and employing a phenomenological and experiential approach, the work rejects ...

Queering Creole Spiritual Traditions: Lesbian, Gay, Bisexual, and Transgender Participation in African-Inspired Traditions in the Americas.(Book Review)

© African Arts December 22, 2004

Queering Creole Spiritual Traditions Lesbian, Gay, Bisexual, and Transgender Participation in African-Inspired Traditions in the Americas.

Randy P. Conner, with David Hatfield Sparks New York: Harrington Press, 2004. 390 pp. $59.95 cloth, $29.95 paper.

As the title indicates, this book is a study of queer practitioners of African-derived spiritual traditions. Relying on both personal experiences with members of these religious communities as well as information gathered from surveys and interviews, the authors conduct a thorough investigation into the participation of lesbian, gay, bisexual, and transgendered/transexual (LGBT) persons in Vodou, Lucumi/Santeria, Candomble, and other spiritual practices inspired by Yoruba religion and philosophy. Rather ...

J. D. Y. Peel, Religious Encounter and the Making of the Yoruba.(Book Review)

© Africa March 22, 2003

J. D. Y. PEEL, Religious Encounter and the Making of the Yoruba. Indianapolis IN: Indiana University Press, 2001, 431 pp. 35.50 [pounds sterling], ISBN 0 253 33794 1.

The 'religious encounter' of the title is that between Christianity, as propagated in Yorubaland (south-western Nigeria) by foreign missionary societies from the 1840s onwards and the religious traditions they encountered locally, which included Islam (introduced into the region a couple of centuries earlier than Christianity) as well as indigenous Yoruba cults. More specifically, the focus of John Peel's book is on one particular missionary body, the Anglican Church Missionary Society; only passing attention is paid here to its Methodist, Baptist and Roman Catholic rivals, or to the 'African Churches' formed by secession from the missions from the 1880s onwards. In terms of its documentary basis, the study rests principally upon a meticulous reading of the voluminous records of the CMS 'Yoruba Mission', and more especially the journals of its local agents; although these are interpreted in the light of twentieth-century anthropological studies . .

A philosophical defence of punishment in traditional African legal culture: the Yoruba example.

© Journal of Pan African Studies September 30, 2009

Introduction

The Yoruba constitute one of the major ethnic groups of modern Nigeria. They effectively occupy the whole of Ogun, Ondo, Oyo, Ekiti, Lagos, and a substantial part of Kwara State (Atanda 1980,1). Aside from Nigeria, the Yoruba are also found in sizeable numbers in the south eastern part of the republic of Benin, Togo, and Dahomey in West Africa, in West India and in South Africa. There is also a thriving Yoruba culture in South America and the Caribbean, especially Brazil and Cuba, where the descendants of the unwilling immigrants to the new world have been able to maintain their identity and preserve their cultural heritage (Gbadegesin 1991,174).While the Yoruba are dispersed throughout the world, this paper focuses on the Nigerian Yoruba. The reason for this choice is that the ancestral home of the Yoruba is in Nigeria and each of the Yoruba in the Diaspora still traces its origin to this home where the culture thrives best.

Yoruba culture is an amalgam of reality permeating all aspects of life, that is, pattern of living and habit of thought of the Yoruba. As a complex whole, Yoruba culture is a composition of knowledge, beliefs, art, moral, religion, customs, politics, technology, law and ...

Traces of Afrocentricity in The Lion and the Jewel and The Road by Wole Soyinka.

© Journal of Pan African Studies June 30, 2012
Introduction

Akivande Oluwole Soyinka was born on the 13th of July in 1934 in Abekuta in the western section of Nigeria; he is a dramatist, poet, novelist, literary critic, theatre director, sometime actor, and the first Nigerian Noble Prize winner for literature in 1986 (Euba 438). He was born in Nigeria to a well-educated family when it was still a British colony; Soyinka has strong feelings and roots in Yoruba culture, an element of life that has filled much of his works (ibid.). Hence, "he seeks to make the worldview of his native Yoruba relevant to his work as an artist who uses Western forms" (George 267).

Soyinka can be considered a victim of colonialism, as he witnessed Europeans trying to change his Yoruba culture to fit their own, thus, he acknowledged the dangers and evils of colonialism concerning every person that has been hurt from colonialism (Wilson). In this regard, Wilson also claims that Soyinka sees the African artistic or cultural essence either absent from or dependent upon Western ideas; which has been forced into silence, but never denied its own being.

According to George, Soyinka intends to show that African people have rich cultural traditions and systems of thoughts that can be ...

African culture and the status of Women: the Yoruba example. (Report)

© Journal of Pan African Studies March 1, 2012
Introduction

Discourse on the rights of women in Africa has been a major focus of contemporary scholarship in Africa. Many scholars of feminist studies have been largely unanimous that aspects of African culture are hostile to women, hence the need for a paradigm shift so that the supposed hitherto marginalised woman will be emancipated, this paper discusses the right of African women in a Yoruba context with emphasis placed on two divides of culture as possible agents of women oppression and therefore, its relevance in promoting rights of women. Hence, this is a way of correcting misconception about culture in relation to the gender question.

Culture has been variously defined; it is understood as a way of life of a people. Thus, culture is made up the customs, traditions, beliefs, behaviour, dress, language, works of art and craft, attitude to life among others, which varies from society to society and suggests that cultural values are largely relative. And similarly, E.B. Tylor has acceptingly defined culture as "That complex whole, which includes knowledge, belief, art, morals, law, custom and any other capabilities and habit acquired by man as a member of society". (Edo 2005:2)
The Woman in Yoruba Culture
The ...

Human personality and the Yoruba worldview: an ethico-sociological interpretation. (Report)

© Journal of Pan African Studies March 15, 2009
Introduction

Our main concern in this paper is to provide an ethico-sociological analysis and interpretation of the idea of human personality in the Yoruba worldview. There is an interesting pool of scholarly literature on human personality in Yoruba thought generated around the philosophical discussions and accounts of what constitute human personality in Yoruba worldview which clearly shows that scholastic concerns have overwhelmingly dwelled on issues dealing with metaphysical interpretations and explanations of destiny, human nature and the reality of human existence. (1)

In many of this earlier metaphysical discourse on human personality, the emphasis and focus have usually been on what constitute the nature of personality. Various interpretations such as monism, dualism, soft-determinism, fatalism and naturalism have been given by scholars. Central to this discourse on the nature of human personality in African thought is the adoption of the comparative methodological approach by scholars viz-a-viz the Western philosophical perspectives.

While the above approach and interpretation are of a truth, of philosophical importance, our focus is to explore another philosophical dimension about human ...

Yoruba traditional medicine and the challenge of integration.

© Journal of Pan African Studies September 30, 2009
Culture as Identity Marker

Culture is the totality of the ways of life of a people and it encompasses the totality of people's beliefs and practices. There are so many cultures in the world which are marked by their distinct qualities. For instance, we have American culture, British culture, Russian culture, etc. In Nigeria also, we have Hausa culture, Igbo culture, Urhobo culture, etc. One prominent of these Nigerian cultures is Yoruba culture which is the concern of this paper. One specific feature of culture is its originality. In this respect, for a way of life of a particular people to be regarded as a culture, it must be devoid of influx from people not of their culture.

Second, Yoruba culture is that it is situated in the metaphysical belief in the supernatural beings such as Olodumare, the Orisas, the oku orun. This marks their belief in two planes of existence; Orun and Aye. Aye (and everything therein including human body and soul) is believed to be created by Olodumare and the Orisas who resides in Orun (1). This informs their belief that the souls of the dead go to Orun, where it came from, to continue to live there. However, the requirement is that these souls must have fulfilled their mission in aye for them to be admitted ...

Socio-cultural and attitudinal study of selected Yoruba taboos in South West Nigeria.(Report)

© Studies in Literature and Language February 29, 2012
INTRODUCTION

Taboo is a major component of the Yoruba culture. It is one way in which the Yoruba society expresses its disapproval of certain kinds of behaviour believed to be harmful to its members, either for supernatural reasons or because such behaviour violates a moral code. In line with this understanding, Osei (2006) posits that "taboos represent the main source of guiding principles regulating and directing the behaviour of individuals and the community towards the Supreme Being and especially the gods and the ancestors in African traditional societies". It is the prohibition against touching, saying, or doing something for fear of immediate harm from a supernatural force. Akindele and Adegbite (1999) further explain that Taboo words and expressions reflect social customs and views of the Yoruba culture. It can be characterized as being concerned with behaviour which is believed to be supernaturally forbidden or regarded as immoral and improper. The term 'taboo' comes from the Tongan word 'tabu', meaning set apart or forbidden.

Every society has a culture and taboos hold the society together. Although some taboos can be traced to apparent danger in health and safety, no common explanation has ...

The Shattered Gourd: Yoruba Forms in Twentieth Century American Art.(Book Review)

© African Arts June 22, 2005
The Shattered Gourd Yoruba Forms in Twentieth Century American Art by Moyo Okediji New York: University of Washington Press, 2003. 202 pp., 46 black and white photos. $40 hardcover.

This is a study of the history of the ways in which modern and contemporary African American artists have drawn, through their art, from Yoruba culture to express their feelings and reactions to their lives in the United States. To do this, Okediji employs two main concepts: counter-hegemony, the artistic reaction to the oppression of African Americans, the active resistance to white domination and racism; and auto-hegemony, art which is oriented towards healing and self-development. For the African American artist, counter-hegemony largely arose in the post-World War II period of racial tensions in the United States; auto-hegemony has had a more recent artistic flourishing, though Okediji sees overlapping trends in individual African American artists. Other concepts that work their way through this volume are amnesia and anamesis, the forgetting of the past (in this case Africa), and its recollection. Re-membering, in the author's usage, essentially represents African Americans' learning of Africa for the first time, in contrast to dismembering, a term ...

African Philosophy: The Analytic Approach

© African Studies Review December 1, 2006
Barry Malien. African Philosophy: The Analytic Approach. Trenton, N.J.: African World Press, 2006. vii + 351 pp. Photographs. Bibliography. Index. $34.95. Paper.

Barry Hallen argues that the analysis of how concepts are used in ordinary language is an essential methodology of analytic philosophy. Such an approach, he maintains, constitutes "African philosophy, insofar as it may deal with the analysis of African languages (or meanings) and the evaluation of African beliefs expressed in these languages" (86). In his view, deriving a philosophy from African languages will not begin until we can correctly understand and translate the relevant meanings. He then applies this method to ...

An interview with Niyi Osundare.(Endangered Languages)(Interview)

© World Literature Today September 1, 2007
Niyi Osundare was born in 1947 in Ikere-Ekiti, Nigeria. He is a poet, dramatist, essayist, critic, and media columnist who has published over ten volumes of poetry, two books of selected poems, four plays, a book of essays, and numerous articles. He has won numerous prizes, among them the Commonwealth Poetry Prize in 1986; the Noma Award; Africa's most prestigious book award; and the Fonlon/ Nichols Award for literary excellence and contribution to human rights in Africa. A survivor of Hurricane Katrina in 2005, he has since returned to the University of New Orleans, where he currently teaches literature and creative writing.

Osundare's numerous travels have influenced him, but it is Nigeria, with its linguistic and cultural diversity, that has most shaped his writing. In his poetry, Osundare draws from the oral tradition of Yoruba, one of the three largest ethnic groups of Nigeria. Because the Yoruba oral tradition is a shared community experience, Osundare emphasizes drama and performance in his own poetry, often reading aloud with audience participation. Though Yoruba is not endangered, the bulk of its literature--like most endangered languages in Africa and elsewhere--is oral. Osundare's eloquent discussion of how that oral ...

Strategic Transformations in Nigerian Writing: Rev. Samuel Johnson, Amos Tutuola, Wole Soyinka, Ben Okri.

© Journal of Asian and African Studies August 1, 1998
Ato Quayson, (Oxford: James Currey & Bloomington: Indiana University Press, 1997), x, 192 pp. Cloth $39.95, paper $17.95.

With this book, Quayson joins in the debate over the problematic issue of paradigms, evolution and originality in African literatures, a topic many critics such as Larson, Irele, Obiechina, Julien, Gates, Appiah, Ngugi, and Mudimbe have discussed at length. His contribution lies in his deviation from the dualistic path often adopted in assessing the relationship between orality and literacy. Instead of stressing the contentious disparity, he foregrounds the correlative interplay between the two trends - interdiscursivity - against the backdrop of a chronological evolution of modern Nigerian literature: orality lent recognizable narrative idiosyncrasies to modern writings. Quayson links Samuel Johnson to Ben Okri through Funguwa, Tutuola and Soyinka. He inscribes his study within a mythopoeic paradigm of which Yoruba culture constitutes the main component and ...

Out of West Africa

© Syracuse New Times July 18, 2007
Out of West Africa

The Eversori Museum explores Yoruba artwork with a religious agenda
The Everson Museum of Art's new exhibit sweeps through two galleries and encompasses 90 pieces including wood sculptures, brass figures, masks and divination trays. African Shapes of the Sacred: Yoruba Religious Art emphasizes essential tenets of Yoruba cosmology, starting with a quest for balance between order and chaos, in relations between men and women, and between the universe's benevolent and malevolent forces.

Yoruba people, who live in the West African nations of Nigeria, Togo and the Republic of Benin, believe in continuous change and transformation, in active ...

Beautiful/Ugly: African and Diaspora Aesthetics

© The International Journal of African Historical Studies January 1, 2007
Beautiful/Ugly: African and Diaspora Aesthetics. Edited by Sarah Nuttal. Prince Claus Fund for Culture and Development. Durham, N.C: Duke University Press, 2006. Pp. 416. $27.95 paper.

Beautiful/Ugly: African and Diaspora Aesthetics, edited by Sarah Nuttal, is an ambitious project that attempts to explore the intersection between Western, Diaspora, and African notions of the beautiful and the ugly through a wide range of topics, places, and media for capturing this elusive meeting point. Quite literally, the more than eighteen essays, by African and Africanist scholars like Gikandi, Mbembe, Barnard, Clarke, and Gevisser, among others, attempt to understand that primal point of ...

Arrest the Music! Fela and His Rebel Art and Politics

© The International Journal of African Historical Studies May 1, 2005
Arrest the Music! Fela and His Rebel Art and Politics. By Tejumola Olaniyan. Bloomington: Indiana University Press, 2004. Pp. x, 242; 13 illustrations. $19.95 paper.

One fascinating paradox of cultural studies is that the elegance of its analysis frequently surpasses the aesthetic distinction of what is being scrutinized. When that occurs, what starts out as a vehicle for extolling popular expression can end up undermining the legitimacy of what is being celebrated. If popular music in Guinea or decorated lorries in Ghana need an academic interlocutor to explain and champion their artistic value to a global audience, than by implication, such forms of popular culture are ...

Santeria Enthroned: Art, Ritual, and Innovation in an Afro-Cuban Religion.(Book review)

© African Arts December 22, 2007
[ILLUSTRATION OMITTED]

Santeria Enthroned: Art, Ritual, and Innovation in an Afro-Cuban Religion by David H. Brown Chicago: University of Chicago Press, 2003. xx + 413 pp. , 27 color, 108 b/w illustrations, notes, glossary, bibliography, index. $95.00 (cloth), $38.00 (softcover).

The Yoruba Diaspora in the Atlantic World Edited by Toyin Falola and Matt D. Childs Bloomington: Indiana University Press, 2004. xii + 455 pp. 12 b/w illustrations, bibliography, index. $70. 00 (cloth), $27.00 (softcover).

From its emergence as a field of inquiry well over one hundred years ago, a body of literature in African Diaspora studies has been focused on the identification of connections between cultural manifestations in Africa and the Americas. David H. Brown's Santeria Enthroned: Art, Ritual, and Innovation in an Afro-Cuban Religion and the edited volume by Toyin Falola and Matt D. Childs titled The Yoruba Diaspora in the Atlantic World both serve as progressive studies that push the field to an even more nuanced exploration of not only the nature, but also the systematic development of "Africanisms" in the trans-Atlantic world. More specifically, the authors explore the construction of an explicitly Yoruba identity ...

Precepts for tenure ethics in Yoruba Egungun (Masquerade) proverbs.(Report)

© Journal of Pan African Studies August 1, 2007
Introduction: Yoruba (1) Egungun Tradition

The Egungun festival (2) is always full of sights and sounds that give immense entertainment to all spectators, both indigenes and visitors in every community where it is held. This is however not what is of real importance in the festival. The artistic aspects (3)--costumes, acrobatics, singing, drumming, dancing, community fellowship, and feasting--important as they are, are not the ultimate function of the Egungun festival among the Yoruba. Thus when attention is carefully paid to the underlying ideas of the festival, it becomes obvious that we ought to go deeper than the artistic surface if we hope to reach and benefit from the social message that the festival strives to portray (4).

In the indigenous thought of the Yoruba, nature consists of spiritual and physical phenomena. And reality, in that worldview, is not partitioned; but rather, there is a permanent continuum between physical reality and spiritual reality. In this way, the two aspects of reality are continuously interacting with one another so it is not often easy to separate them in thought and in practice. An aspect of this idea of nature is the entrenched belief that physical death is not the cessation of life for ...

THE CENTRALITY OF WOMEN IN MORAL TEACHINGS IN YORUBA FAMILY SYSTEM

© Gender & Behaviour June 1, 2011
Abstract

Social order and peaceful co-existence are some of the primary goals in every human society. To have these and other conditions which ensure lives and properties secured, societies ensure moral and ethical uprightness of its members. This is done through various social institutions - Family, Education, and Marriage to mention a few. Among the Yoruba people of south Western Nigeria, parents and other family members are the first teachers of their children, instructing them in the "proper" ways of life approved by the society. For example, relating with elders and people of same age group, humility, diligence, truthful and accommodating. Culturally among the Yoruba ...

Mapping Yorùbá Networks: Power and Agency in the Making of Transnational Communities

© The International Journal of African Historical Studies January 1, 2005
Mapping Yorùbá Networks: Power and Agency in the Making of Transnational Communities. By Kamari Maxine Clarke. Durham: Duke University Press, 2004. Pp. xxix, 345. $22.95 paper.

In Oyotunji Village, South Carolina, residents speak Yoruba, respect the rule of an oba, and practice the religion of the orishas. They are all of American origin, but they identify as African, and particularly as Yoruba people whose ancestors were forcibly relocated across the Atlantic. Oyotunji Village, founded in 1970, represents their efforts to claim this identity and to create a physical, political, social, and economic space where they can follow what they see as Yoruba "traditions."

In this ...

Yinka Shonibare: Double Dutch. (Book Review)

© African Arts June 22, 2005
Yinka Shonibare Double Dutch
Edited by Jaap Guldemond and Gabriele Mackert, with Barbera van Kooij
Rotterdam: NAi Publishers, 2004. 160 pp., 75 color and 25 b/w photos, biography, bibliography. $39.95 softcover.

In just over a decade of artistic practice, Yinka Shonibare has captured and retained the attention of the contemporary Western art scene with his eye-catching headless mannequins and engaging photo narratives. This London-based artist of Yoruba heritage addresses contemporary issues of globalization and the colonial past with a light-heartedness that has won him universal appeal.

Yinka Shonibare: Double Dutch contains the most comprehensive look at the artist's work to date. Lavishly illustrated with works spanning Shonibare's career (1994-2004), the colorful exhibit catalogue effectively reproduces the experience of coming face to face with Shonibare's whimsical and vibrant works. Punctuated by a diverse assortment of scholarly articles, the catalogue is a treat for the intellect as well as the eye.

The collection of seven articles six ...

Fashioning Africa: Power and Politics of Dress.

© African Arts December 22, 2008
Fashioning Africa: Power and Politics of Dress
ed. by Jean Allman
Indiana University Press, 2004; 256 pages, 36 b&w photos, index. $50 cloth; $21.95 paper
[ILLUSTRATION OMITTED]

Jean Allman's edited volume on African dress adds substantially to research on dress as nonverbal communication with its focus on power and politics. The book is a gem. I followed its development from attendance at the two panels of papers presented at the 2001 African Studies Association meetings to its publication in 2004, assigning it for my seminar on Dress and Culture, where it stimulated lively discussion. The chapter contributors are interdisciplinary, dominated by seven historians, followed by two anthropologists, an art historian, a dress scholar, and a communications specialist. Allman selected several writers already known to Africanists as having published books or articles on African dress, such as Judith Byfield (2002), Margaret Jean Hay (1992, 1996), Elisha Renne Q995), Victoria Rovine (2001), and Phyllis Martin (1996). Newcomers are Heather Akou, Marissa Moorman, Andrew Ivaska, and Boatema Boateng.

Allman's phrase "the sartorial study of power" (p. 4) succinctly introduces the common issues featured in the chapters. As a historian who ...

A Director's Vision for Theater in Africa: Adeniyi Coker Interviews Ola Rotimi -- One of Nigeria's Foremost Playwrights and Directors

© Black Renaissance/Renaissance Noire July 1, 2003
On Beginning a Career in Nigeria
Adeniyi Coker: How did it all begin for you?
Ola Rotimi: I got to Ife in 1966 after graduating from Yale, and when I arrived at Ife there wasn't any active theater unit -- that is to say, active in the sense of producing plays, which of

course is the ultimate goal of any theater unit. There was a research fellowship position in drama at the Institute of African studies, which I filled, and being an active theater man I could not just carry on researching without doing some practice. So I went on staging plays on the side with funds from the Institute of African Studies. That was how I was able to stage my first play, Our Husband has gone Mad …

A Companion to African Philosophy

© African Studies Review September 1, 2004
SCIENCE & PHILOSOPHY Kwasi Wiredu, ed. A Companion to African Philosophy. Maiden, Mass.: Blackwell Publishing, Ltd., 2004. 587 pp. Bibliography. Index. $124.95. Cloth.

Few books focus on African philosophy. Indeed, some outside of Africa are "surprise [d] at the mention of African philosophy" (xix), assuming that it is a Western construct. In his one-volume Companion to African Philosophy, Kwasi Wiredu has gathered forty-two well-researched and enlightening essays on the subject by both well-known and unknown sages, philosophers, academics, and politicians. Intended to form a comprehensive text on African philosophy for a target audience of graduate or undergraduate students, …

Architect On New Black History Museum Design

© NPR All Things Considered February 22, 2012 Melissa Block
All Things Considered
02-22-2012

Host: The new museum will be 374,000 square feet, right next to the Washington Monument. It was designed by three architects. And the architect of record on the project joins me here in the studio. Philip Freelon, welcome to the program.MELISSA BLOCK
Time 21:00-22:00 PM

Play Audio

MELISSA BLOCK, host: The new museum will be 374,000 square feet, right next to the Washington Monument. It was designed by three architects. And the architect of record on the project joins me here in the studio. Philip Freelon, welcome to the program.

PHILIP FREELON: Thank you for …

Ewe: The Use of Plants in Yoruba Society.

© Africa March 22, 1997
Pierre Verger (`Fatumbi is a title given him by Yoruba sacred men and women'), who died in 1995, aged 92, was born in France and spent many years studying Yoruba epistemology and medicine, in Benin and in Nigeria. He later lived in Brazil, where he made comparative studies of these topics in Bahia. This book summarises his life's work.

The book is in three parts, the first examining Yoruba plant classification and main beliefs regarding illness and other evils and how to deal with them. The second part (comprising 80 per cent of the text) provides 447 `Magical and Medical Formulae'. `If western medicine prioritizes a plant's scientific name and its pharmacological …

Take the power back: Rita Indiana y Los Misterios reveal Dominican music's roots.(GENF)

© The Fader April 1, 2010
In a recent photo, Rita Indiana has a plush stuffed kitten perched in a basket on her head and is smoking a cigarillo. Two swoops of hot pink eyeshadow jet across her lids, and there's a tattoo of two triangles on her wifebeat-er-bared shoulder that looks like a fast-forward button. She is Carmen Miranda, Wendy O. Williams and gangster supermodel all in one--a protean confluence of identities Indiana channels through the vibrance of her feral electro-mambo band, Los Misterios.
[ILLUSTRATION OMITTED]
The path to her radical status comes from surprising origins, though. By the time she was 20, Indiana was already a star in her native Dominican Republic on the …

Orisha

© Encyclopedia of African-American Culture and History January 1, 2006
African traditional religions became the foundation of new religions created out of the experience of Africans in the Americas. Variously called Vodou (Haiti), Santería (Cuba), Candomblé (Brazil), and Orisha (Trinidad), these religions developed in response to the physical, social, and spiritual oppression of slavery and its aftermath. They are as much systems of resistance, retention, and creative adaptation as they are religions. Their persistence and progress into the twenty-first century represent an account of the irrepressible will of the human spirit in the story of Africans in the diaspora.

The term *orisha* refers to the deities of the Yoruba pantheon. According to Bolaji Idowu (1994), the word is a composite of two ideas: *ori*, "head," and *se*, …

Stout, Reneé

© Encyclopedia of African-American Culture and History January 1, 2006
1958
Reneé Stout was born in Junction City, Kansas, and grew up in Pittsburgh, Pennsylvania. When she was ten years old, Stout attended Saturday art classes at the Carnegie Museum of Art, where she encountered an object in the museum collection that, combined with her fascination with a mysterious spiritualist who had a consultation space in her neighborhood, had a profound effect upon the nature of her mature artwork. The object was an African nail figure by the Bakongo (or Kongo) people of Central Africa called a *nkisi nkondi*. The spiritualist was Madam Ching, and though Stout never actually talked with her, the mystery of …

Oyeyemi, Helen 1984–

© Contemporary Authors January 1, 2006
PERSONAL: Born 1984, in Nigeria; brought to England, c. 1988; father a teacher, mother a worker in the London

subways. *Education:* Attended Corpus Christi College, Cambridge.

ADDRESSES: Agent—c/o Author Mail, Nan A. Talese, 1745 Broadway, New York, NY 10019.

CAREER: Writer.

WRITINGS:

The Icarus Girl (fiction), Nan A. Talese (New York, NY), 2005.

Also author of plays *Juniper's Whitening* and *Victimese.*

WORK IN PROGRESS: A novel about Cuban mythology; a volume of plays.

SIDELIGHTS: Helen Oyeyemi wrote her first novel, *The Icarus Girl*, in seven months, and by the time she was nineteen years old …

Obasanjo, Nigeria and the world. (Brief article)(Book review)

© Reference & Research Book News December 1, 2011
9781847010278
Obasanjo, Nigeria and the world.
Iliffe, John.
James Currey Publishers
2011
326 pages
$80.00
Hardcover
DT515

This is a biography of Olusegun Obasanjo, the military ruler of Nigeria from 1976 to 1979 and president from 1999 to 2007. Attempting to resolve the contradiction between Obasanjo's many achievements as a soldier and statesman and the obloquy that was visited upon his …

Holiday lobster recipes. (includes recipes from three African American chefs)

© American Visions December 1, 1993
The holidays are filled with tradition, sharing and pleasant surprises. In continuing the tradition of sharing favorite holiday recipes, American Visions considers the choices of three individuals who, although they excel at their craft and although their creations are well-received, are largely unseen and unknown executive chefs at elegant restaurants.

"It was in the blood, I guess," says Patrick Clark, the 38-year-old executive chef of the Lafayette Restaurant at the Hay-Adams Hotel in Washington, D.C. Clark, whose father was also a chef, has been around the kitchen since he was about 10 years old.

Before arriving at the Hay-Adams in late 1992, he studied at the Technical College in his native New York City, then at the Technical College in Bournemouth, England. After working with prominent chefs in London and in Enghien-les-Bains, France, Clark returned to New York in the late 1970s and began his career at Regine's Restaurant. It was, however, at the Odeon Restaurant, a venue for contemporary food that he opened in New York in 1980, that Clark made his name.

Recognition is nothing new to Clark's work space at the Lafayette Restaurant, an open, airy room with a sense of intimacy and a continental flair. Clark is also getting …

Namsifueli Nyeki: a Tanzanian potter extraordinaire.(Critical essay)

© African Arts March 22, 2007

In the highland town of Lushoto, in the Usambara Mountains of northeastern Tanzania, a market day rarely passes without local potters parading into town carrying loads of earthenware on their heads. Although those who are not regular visitors to the weekly markets in the district might claim that one pot looks just like another, to the insider each vessel bears the unmistakable imprint of its maker. "Each potter has her own hand" explains Namsifueli Nyeki, "each potter's village has its own style:" (1) But even to the untrained eye, the unique pottery of Namsifueli herself (FIG. 1) clearly stands out from other potters. Although her work is grounded in the long-standing pottery traditions of her ancestors, Namsifueli's interest in experimentation, new designs, and individualized detailing lend her work (FIG. 2) the distinct touch of an artist unconstrained by the limitations of mila, or cultural tradition. (2) As such, she poses an interesting contradiction to notions of anonymity, conformity, and conservatism in African pottery. This essay therefore follows in the footsteps of important, though infrequent, studies conducted from the 1950s to 1970s on individual potters, which introduced notions of individuality and authorship in African ceramics and the names of African …

A syntactic and semiotic analysis of some Yoruba sexist proverbs in English translation: need for gender balance.

© Nebula September 1, 2007
Abstract

Using systemic, structural and contrastive linguistic theories as bases of analysis, the paper identifies and explicates eighteen English-translated Yoruba proverbs associated with women and brings out their inadequacies with regard to gender prejudice against the female race. Out of the eighteen, fourteen are found to be gender-biased while only four of them are gender-neutral and can apply to both sexes. From the foregoing, the paper suggests the second versions of these proverbs that cater for the gender not represented in the first set. Thus, the paper is able to prove that the same set of proverbs can be used as reprimand for both the female and male sexes and not for only one of them as they were originally.

Introduction

Just like among many races of the world, the Yoruba people of the southwestern geopolitical zone of Nigeria hold the use of proverbs in esteem. This is to the extent that there are different sets of proverbs that accompany various human activities, events, things and ideas (Daramola, 2004; Salami, 2004 and Asiyanbola, 2006). Although some scholars look at proverbs as being archaic and moribund, nowadays; some of these so-called archaic proverbs, which are legacies of …

Art, exile and resistance: an interview with Wole Soyinka. (playwright and activist)(Interview)

© American Theatre January 1, 1997

Even the briefest of encounters with Wole Soyinka - celebrated playwright, essayist, activist and winner of the 1986 Nobel Prize for Literature - is enough to make evident the qualities that are at the crux of his accomplishments. A formidable and centered man, he speaks with a quiet and utter confidence - a confidence that belies his personal fury for the events of June 12, 1993, which rendered him into exile from his native Nigeria.

It was on that day that a military coup prevented a newly elected civilian government from assuming power. Large numbers of Nigerians had voted across ethnic and regional lines in what was widely seen as the country's most democratic election ever - an event that, in Soyinka's eyes, was his homeland's last best hope of becoming a free and viable nation. But the military strongman Gen. Ibrahim Babangida, who had ruled Nigeria for eight years (in the process building one of Africa's largest private fortunes), forbade publication of the voting results and, in place of the election's ostensible winner, installed his own deputy, the brutal Gen. Sani Abacha, as head of state. Soyinka celebrated his 60th birthday with a protest march against Abacha's takeover, an action that led to threats of house arrest and ...

Me and My Shadow

© Black Issues Book Review November 1, 2005
Me and My Shadow

A remarkable first novel from a young Brit haunts the mind and soul.

Can a writer step out of herself and write a novel? Helen Oyeyemi, author of the novel The Icarus Girl, says she did just that.

"The best part of The Icarus Girl was leaving myself behind and imagining, taking a diasporic look at Nigerian myth and this strong, brave, whimsical, precocious little girl that I wanted to get to know," Oyeyemi says.

Writers often talk about holding conversations with their characters. Some authors even wonder where their stories come from. But if the story isn't from the author, well, where is it from? Is it possible for a writer to be haunted? Of ...

An Egyptian in China: Ahmed Fahmy and the making of "world Christianities".(Biography)

© Church History June 1, 2009
"In my early years in Changchow there were still some of Dr. Fahmy's students in practice in the town, and plenty of people, patients and church members, who remembered him with much gratitude and affection. I think you will be glad to know that ... there will also be people in Changchow who never knew Dr. Fahmy but who nevertheless will be giving thanks for the work which he started and from which they and many others have benefited over the years."

--D. J. Harman to Mrs. Johnston (granddaughter of Ahmed Fahmy), dated Eltham, London, November 14, 1987

I. AHMED FAHMY IN THE MISSIONARY CONTEXT

Ahmed Fahmy, who was born in Alexandria, Egypt, in 1861 and died in Golders Green, London, in 1933, (1) was the most celebrated convert from Islam to Christianity in the history of the American Presbyterian mission in Egypt. American Presbyterians had started work in Egypt in 1854 and soon developed the largest Protestant mission in the country. (2) They opened schools, hospitals, and orphanages; sponsored the development of Arabic Christian publishing and Bible distribution; and with local Egyptians organized evangelical work in towns and villages from Alexandria to Aswan. In an age when Anglo-American Protestant missions were ...

Funerals and Burial Ceremonies

© World Eras January 1, 2004
Sources

Rituals for Young People. In Africa, as in other cultures, a death in the family was probably the most painful experience for the members of the clan. The death of an elder called for an elaborate celebration, which in some instances—as in the Yoruba culture—might last for several months. When a younger family member died, however, the cause of death was investigated. If the medicine men determined that the person did not die of natural causes, the village had to embark on elaborate rituals to ascertain who was responsible for the untimely death. The dead body was left for several days while the village ...

Nov. 19-25

© New Orleans CityBusiness November 19, 2007
Nov. 19

A Post-Katrina Crime Mystery, 7 p.m. at the Jefferson Parish East bank Regional Library, 4747 W. Napoleon Ave. in Metairie. Author Eric Spindler will discuss and read from her novel "Last Known Victim." A question and answer session and book signing will follow the discussion. Copies of "Last Known Victim" will be available for purchase through Friends of Jefferson Public Library. The event is free and open to the public. Registration is not necessary. For more information, visit www.jefferson.lib.la.us or contact Jim Davis, adult programming manager, at 838-1100.

Nov. 20

Looking Back at Aug. 29, 2005 An Artist's View of New Orleans Before and After Katrina, ...

Ezenwa-Ohaeto. Winging Words: Interviews with Nigerian Writers and Critics.(Book Review)

© World Literature Today September 1, 2005
Ezenwa-Ohaeto. Winging Words: Interviews with Nigerian Writers and Critics. Ibadan, Nigeria. Kraft (African Books Collective, distr.). 2004 ([c] 2003). 172 pages. 11.95 [pounds sterling]/$24.95. ISBN 978-039-090-1

WINGING WORDS contains interviews with twenty-one Nigerians, classified either as "writers" (John Munonye, Flora Nwapa, Ken Saro-Wiwa, I.N.C. Aniebo, Ifeoma Okoye, Obiora Udechukwu, Eddie Iroh, Niyi Osundare, Zulu Sofola, Chukwuemeka Ike, and Tanure Ojaide) or as "writer/critics" (D. I. Nwoga, Ernest Emenyonu, Kalu Uka, Isidore Okpewho, Dan

Izevbaye, Charles Nnolim, Chinweizu, Edith Ihekweazu, Ossie Enekwe, and Sunday Anozie). All the interviews were ...

Flava: Wedge Curatorial Projects 1997-2007.(Book review)

© African Arts September 22, 2009
Flava: Wedge Curatorial Projects 1997-2007

Edited by Elizabeth Harney

Toronto: Wedge Curatorial Projects, 2008. 142 pp., 50 color and 80 b&w photos, index. $60 cloth.

[ILLUSTRATION OMITTED]

Flava: Wedge Curatorial Projects (1997-2007) presents a collection of photographic images exploring issues related to black identity and culture. The photographs, taken in Diaspora communities around the globe, range from the post-World War I era to the present day. The book is introduced by Deborah Willis, leading historian of African American photography, and edited by Elizabeth Harney. It celebrates the vision of Dr. Kenneth Montague, director of Wedge Curatorial Projects, a Toronto-based photographic gallery whose curatorial mission is "dedicated to photo based work exploring black identity" (jacket notes). Flava--an expression used by photographer Jamel Shabazz, whose street images of 1980s New York hip-hop culture are featured prominently in the book--comes from the African American lexicon and refers to the essential element or flavor found in relevant cultural expression ...

Nothing About Us Without Us: Disability Oppression and Empowerment.

© The Progressive July 1, 1998
Nothing About Us Without Us: Disability Oppression and Empowerment by James I. Charlton University of California Press. 247 pages. $27.50

James Charlton, a longtime disability-rights activist, traveled around the world in the 1980s and 1990s to study from street level the depth of poverty and difficult conditions among people with disabilities, as well as the spirit of those who are working to change things. The word that best encompasses the status of people with disabilities worldwide--in capitalist systems and otherwise--is "outcasts," Charlton says.

The extent and form of our banishment varies widely. In some African countries, he reports, kids with ...

Symptoms and strangeness in Yoruba anti-aesthetics. (Emerging Scholarship in African Art)

© African Arts December 22, 2005
Bi oju ko ba rohun bi okun Oju o le rohun bi i ide (If the eyes have not seen a thing like rope, The eyes cannot see a thing like bronze.)
--Chief Agbongbon Inaolaji of Ilora (September 3, 1998)
Receiving, giving, giving, receiving, all that lives is twin. Who would cast the spell of death, let him separate the two.
--Ayi Kwei Armah (1973:xi)

When I arrived in Nigeria for my third visit in 1998--a time then widely regarded as the lowest moment in that country's history--the celebration of classicizing grace that colored Yoruba art historical scholarship of the 1960s, 1970s, and 1980s seemed pretty much out of the question. This was the Nigeria of General Sani Abacha, a president considered by most Nigerians to be a despot, a thief, and a murderer. After taking power in 1994, Abacha instituted self-serving political and economic programs that plunged Nigeria into profound disintegration. When Death came for Abacha in June 1998, the naira, once valued at two US dollars, was worth about a penny. Universities were drastically underfunded, prompting strikes by students and professors alike. The national electrical and communications utilities were crumbling, and a relentless government-manufactured shortage of ...

Rape-related English and Yoruba proverbs.

© Women and Language September 22, 1998
Introduction

A proverb has been defined as a short, repeated, witty statement or set of statements of wisdom, truth and experience which is used to further a social end (see Mieder 1989a; Seitel 1981; Egblewogbe 1980). About the truth of proverbs, Kirshenblatt-Gimblett (1973:821) notes, following Malof (1966), that

Neat symmetries and witty convergences of sound and meaning, tight formulations of logical relations, highly patterned repetitions, structural balance, and familiar metaphors encapsulate general principles and contribute to the feeling that anything that sounds so right must be true.

She states that, contrary to this feeling, a proverb "expresses relative rather than absolute truths" (p. 821). She justifies this claim with the fact a proverb may express more than one meaning which may contradict one another.

According to Albig (1931:529), "the proverb is a social definition of a situation." Oduyoye (1979:5) also notes that "proverbs, aphorisms and other pithy sayings serve as socialisation maxims." Similarly, Page and Washington (1987:50) observe that

Once internalized, proverbs, like values, become unconscious as well as conscious standards for action and attitudes toward self and others ... Proverbs, like values, protect the ...

Yoruba Girl Dancing and the Post-War Transition to an English Multi-Ethnic Society

© Ethnic Studies Review January 1, 1999
This paper exemplifies the insider/outsider binary in a nation's shift towards a multi-ethnic society. The writer gives insight into the African Diaspora within England in her exploration of Yoruba Girl Dancing.

Simi Bedford's Yoruba Girl Dancing tells the story of Remi Foster, a small Nigerian girl who is uprooted in the early 1950s from her large and ebullient Yoruba family and transplanted to England. There she attends an exclusive English boarding school and spends vacations in suburbia with her step-grandmother's white relatives. Remi's is the story of a reluctant pioneer in the post-war process whereby urban England gradually became a multi-ethnic society and received the ...

Photography's other histories. (General)(Book Review)

© Journal of the Royal Anthropological Institute September 1, 2004
PINNEY, CHRISTOPHER & NICOLAS PETERSON (eds). Photography's other histories. viii, 286 pp., illus., bibliogr. London, Durham: Duke Univ. Press, 2003. [pounds sterling]17.95 (paper)

Photography has long been a tool of the ethnographer. However, it has also been used by the media in conveying popular and distorted images of the exotic 'Other' to a European audience. This collected work, a project that began with an international conference at the Museum of Queensland, Brisbane, in late 1997, aims to present photography as an 'account of a globally disseminated and locally appropriated medium' (p. 1). Photography's other histories should be considered an important contribution to the anthropological literature, since relatively few anthropological studies of ...

The Palm-Wine Drinkard and His Dead Palm-Wine Tapster in the Deads' Town

© World Literature and Its Times: Profiles of Notable Literary Works and the Historic Events That Influenced Them January 1, 2000
by Amos Tutuola
  THE LITERARY WORK
  A novel set in Nigeria in the timeless folkloric past; published in English in 1952.
  SYNOPSIS
  Drinkard, the protagonist and narrator of the novel, goes in search of his deceased palm-wine tapster in Deads' Town. On the way he meets with a series of adventures, in the process gaining a wife and wisdom.
  Events in History at the Time of the Novel
  The Novel in Focus
  For More Information

Born in 1929 in western Nigeria, Amos Tutuola achieved only a sixth-grade education due to financial constraints following his father's death. He later tried his hand at farming, without success, then pursued the blacksmith trade. He served as a coppersmith in the West African Air Corps of the British military in World War II. After the war Tutuola had to take a job as a messenger, and it gave him time, between errands, to write down stories he had heard. His first novel, *The Palm-Wine Drinkard and His Dead Palm-Wine Tapster in the Deads' Town*, became the subject of much controversy because of its frequently ungrammatical, though stylish and vivid, writing. A landmark work, it was the first novel to be ...

The Oriki of a Grasshopper and Other Plays.

© World Literature Today January 1, 1997
Femi Osofisan's prolific career, experimentation with form, ideological commitment, and profundity of themes, plus the sheer poetry of his drama, have distinguished him as without doubt the leading dramatist of the generation of African writers following Wole Soyinka and Chinua Achebe. The publication of The Oriki of a Grasshopper and Other Plays will expose to the wider world a highly talented African dramatist influenced by both traditional Yoruba culture and Western - particularly French - dramaturgy. The four plays in the book reflect not only Osofisan's individual development and talent but also the general mood and direction of contemporary African drama.

I reread the title play one day after ...

In Africa's Forest and Jungle: Six Years Among the Yorubas. (Book review)

© Baptist History and Heritage March 22, 2011
In Africa's Forest and Jungle: Six Years Among the Yorubas. By Richard Henry Stone. Edited by Betty Finklea Florey. Tuscaloosa: University of Alabama Press, 2010. 202 pp.

This book is largely a reprint of an 1899 memoir, written in clear if unremarkable prose by former Southern Baptist Convention (SBC) missionary Richard Stone. It also includes journal entries and letters that Stone composed between 1858 and 1888, which provide a useful complement to the memoir. The book will appeal primarily to scholars focused on Protestant mission efforts in the nineteenth century or to those researching the history of the Yoruba people of West Africa.

Richard and Sue Stone set ...

Asen and methodology in art history.(dialogue)

© African Arts September 22, 2007
The short article on asen by Edna Bay (African Arts vol. 40, no. 1, pp. 6-8), after her analysis of Suzanne Blier's contribution to a catalogue, is, in fact, an invitation to give careful thought to methods used in art history in general and to how we, as art historians, use data collected from the field, in particular. My contribution to this dialogue will focus on four main points, based on my reading of Edna Bay's text:

Art History and History

The present dialogue gains in focus if we first situate it in its global context. As far as I can understand and based on the few pages I have read over the years, there is no formal wall between our science and history, since art history is primarily concerned with creativity, a human process targeting a whole range of expression throughout history. One should, therefore, admit art history as part of general history. As such, most of the methods used by historians are useful to art historians, all of whom are ...

Fast food in Ibadan: an emerging consumption pattern.(Report)

© Africa March 22, 2009
ABSTRACT

In its modernization garb, development has come to mean the inculcation of foreign values resulting in the fundamental transformation of modernizing nations. Ironically, little attention is being drawn to the consequences of modernizing influences. This is the cote of the article. Through qualitative research methodology consisting of in-depth interviews (IDIs), participant observation and informal interviews, the article examines the emergence and ascendancy of fast foods in Ibadan, Nigeria. Our finding is that the middle class, the youth and children, as conveyors of imported cultures (into which they have been socialized), are the major customers whose values are projected through marketing strategies by the fast food outfits. Unfortunately, the health implications of these foods have not been properly grasped by these consumers, and neither have the market operators attempted to sensitize them. The article concludes that even when modernization influences are to be incorporated in the globalizing world, their initiatives must be well contextualized, comprehended and their contours managed for objective development to be achieved and sustained.

RESUME

Sous son apparence de modernisation, le developpement designe desormais l'inculcation de ...

African oral arts in excilia Saldana's Kele kele

© Afro - Hispanic Review April 1, 2002
It is an accepted fact that African cultural practices have greatly influenced life in the Caribbean. As a prominent Caribbean scholar remarks, "African culture not only crossed the Atlantic, it crossed, survived and creatively adapted itself to its new environment" (Brathwaite 73).1 In the case of Cuba, the dominant ethnic group which came from Africa was the Yoruba of Nigeria, whose religious practices are still alive on the island. The Yoruba became known in Cuba as lucumi, their religion became known as santeria, their deities, or orishas, are active in the lucumi religious pantheon, and remnants of the Yoruba language are still heard on the island.2 As William Bascom notes, it is in ...

Ghana: Kufuor Volume II

© New African January 1, 2007
Ghana Kufuor Volume II

The second edition of President John Kufuor's biography, Between Faith and History, will be launched in Accra on 10 January. has been reading it.

Ghana will be awash with a plethora of activities in 2007 as it marks 50 years of independence and post-colonial rule. Throughout the coming year, attention will be focused, to a large extent, on the heroes of the independence struggle, particularly Dr Kwame Nkrumah, the charismatic leader of the African decolonisation period, and also Dr J.B. Danquah, Paa Grant, Ako Adjei, William Ofori-Atta and Obetsebi-Lamptey who make up the popularly remembered 'Big Six' who started the United Gold Coast Convention of ...

The oral traditions in Ile-Ife; the Yoruba people and their book of enlightenment.(Brief article)(Book review)

© Reference & Research Book News February 1, 2010
9781933146652

The oral traditions in Ile-Ife; the Yoruba people and their book of enlightenment.
Ogunyemi, Yemi D.
Academica Press, LLC
2010
176 pages
$74.95
Hardcover
GR351

In order to explore the oral traditions in Ile-Ife, the political, economic and cultural capital of the Yoruba people in the Southwest of what is now known as Nigeria, Yemi D. Ogunyemi, a poet, novelist and scholar of the African Literatures in Africa and in Diaspora, has produced a classical research ...

The Art of Attire

© World Eras January 1, 2004
Sources

Cloth Weaving. Archaeological and historical evidence suggests that the domestic cultivation of cotton and cloth weaving evolved around the third or second millennium B.C.E. in the middle Nile region. By the beginning of the Common Era both cotton and ceramic technologies had also developed in the Western Sudanic and Atlantic areas of West Africa. These technologies were passed on through guild systems. Young apprentices learned not only

[Image not available for copyright reasons]

the skills necessary to practice the craft but also the taboos associated with protecting them. As weaving became an art, various ethnic cultures developed distinctive styles. Historical and archaeological records suggest that cloth weaving began with the use of raffia, specially treated fibers made from the back of a tree called the raffia palm. Raffia cloth was followed by woven strips of cotton and other fibers. Archaeological evidence dates the use of these textiles in West Africa at least back to the eleventh century, when woven cloths were used in funerary rites in the area around the Bandiagara cliffs in present-day Mali. From Senegambia to the Niger long strips of cloth in diverse ...

Olorun

© U*X*L Encyclopedia of World Mythology January 1, 2009
Nationality/Culture
    West African/Yoruba
Pronunciation
    ch-loh-RUN
Alternate Names
    Olofin-Orun, Oba-Orun, Olodumare
Appears In
    Yoruba creation myths
Lineage
    None

Character Overview

In the mythology of the Yoruba people of West Africa, Olorun is the most powerful and wisest god. The all-knowing Olorun takes an active role in the affairs of both heaven and earth. Head of the Yoruba pantheon (or collection of recognized gods), Olorun is also known as Olofin-Orun (Lord of Heaven), Oba-Orun (King of the Sky), and Olodumare (Almighty).

Major Myths

According to Yoruba legend, Olorun was one of ...

Books received.

© Philosophy East and West January 1, 2002

African Philosophy and the Quest for Autonomy: A Philosophical Investigation. By Leonhard Praeg. Amsterdam; Atlanta, Georgia: Editions Rodopi B.V. , 2000. Pp. xxxi + 322. Paper HFL 140, U.S. $60.00.

An Anthology of Philosophy in Persia. Edited by Seyyed Hossein Nasr with Mehdi Aminrazavi. New York: Oxford University Press, 2001. Pp. xv + 400. Hardcover $74.00.

Being Human: Ethics, Environment, and Our Place in the World. By Anna L. Peterson. Berkeley: University of California Press, 2001. Pp. x + 289. Hardcover U.S. $50.00, U.K. 33.50 [pounds sterling]. Paper U.S. $18.95, U.K. 12.50 [pounds sterling].

Cheng-Zhu Confucianism in the Early Qing: Li Guangdi (1642-1718) and Qing Learning. By On-cho Ng. Albany: State University of New York Press, 2001. Pp. ix + 258. Paper $22.95.

Chinese. By Oliver Moore. Berkeley: University of California Press, 2000. Pp. 80. Paper $13.95.

Classical Indian Philosophy of Mind: The Nyaya Dualist Tradition. By Kisor Kumar …

Crossings (exhibition).

© Parachute: Contemporary Art Magazine July 1, 1999

National Gallery of Canada, Ottawa, August 7 - November 1

The Cuban ethnologist Fernando Ortiz uses the word sincretismo to refer to the concept where two or more cultural grounds mesh to produce another entity. While the cultural grounds in "Crossings" synchronize in the sense of coexisting, there is little sense of facile cooperation between them. This is precisely the strength of the exhibition as it derives a charged energy from necessary abstruseness as a result of failed authenticity. The "crossings" represented by these fifteen artists are, as curator Diana Nemiroff suggests in the catalogue, "locale-creating bridge[s] in a contemporary world of shifting frontiers and entangled identities" (p. 39). Although new locales might be created through these works, they are far from essentialist manifestations of home, origin or place. While most of these artists are living and working in a place …

The Yoruba Diaspora in the Atlantic World.(Book review)

© The Historian December 22, 2006

The Yoruba Diaspora in the Atlantic World. Edited by Toyin Falola and Matt D. Childs. (Bloomington, Ind.: Indiana University Press, 2004. Pp. xii, 455. $27.95.)

One of the most important themes in African diaspora historiography is the Yoruba diaspora. Although the subject of the Yoruba has generated an impressive list of academic publications over the years, we are still a long way from a full understanding of the Yoruba dimension of the African diaspora in the Atlantic world. This study is a welcome contribution to this academic effort. The editors must be commended for this impressive volume.

Following a very useful introduction on methodology and research …

Religious Encounter and the Making of the Yoruba.(Brief Article)

© International Bulletin of Missionary Research July 1, 2002

By J. D. Y. Peel. Bloomington: Indiana Univ. Press, 2000. Pp. xi, 420. $49.95.

Since the era of European colonialism, anthropologists have been numbered among the fiercest critics of Christian missions. One great exception has been J. D. Y. Peel, an anthropologist-turned-historian who is presently associated with the School of Oriental and African Studies in London. Peel's most recent book, Religious Encounter and the Making of the Yoruba, is arguably the first great piece of historical writing on the implantation of Christianity in Africa of the twenty-first century. Making use of the letters and reports of Church Missionary Society agents, Peel constructs a …

On Ouidah asen.(dialogue)(West African art)(Critical essay)

© African Arts March 22, 2007

In 1989 Suzanne Preston Blier published an article based on her close reading of the field materials compiled by Melville and Frances Herskovits during their 1931 sojourn in Dahomey. Received negatively by some of Herskovits's close scholarly descendants and admirers, the article nevertheless was a useful addition to scholarship on southern Benin, for it put valuable perspective on the field research methods used by one of the foundational scholars of Dahomean studies, widely hailed as the father of African studies. For those of us who had followed Herskovits into the Dahomean field and used his extensive writings on Dahomey as a guide, Blier's comments helped to clarify inconsistencies; it became apparent that Herskovits's shortcomings were the product of an extraordinarily brief but intense field experience.

Herskovits's work is but one of literally hundreds of extant sources on Dahomey, one of the most richly documented areas of Africa. The Dahomean literature is now enlarged by contributions that Blier and others, including myself, have added. Both Blier and I have carried out continuing archival and field research on the area of the former kingdom of Dahomey over roughly the same academic generation (Blier starting in 1984 and I in 1971). As scholars who have worked ...

African Gender Studies. A Reader

© Gender Forum April 1, 2006

Review: Oyèrónké Oyewùmí, ed. African Gender Studies. A Reader. New York: Palgrave Macmillan, 2005.

With the performative turn's emphasis on the discursive construction of gender categories, a growing awareness has emerged within the interdisciplinary field of gender studies that "insistence on coherence and unity of the category [woman, SA] refuse[s] the multiplicity of cultural, social and political intersections in which the concrete array of 'women' are constructed" (Butler 1990:

14). Hence, the project of countering the internal structure of white hegemony in the field of gender studies - although well under way for considerable time - has gained added momentum and amplified ...

Aspects of Africanness in August Wilson's drama: reading 'The Piano Lesson' through Wole Soyinka's drama.

© African American Review March 22, 1996

The experimental flourish of the Counterculture and Civil Rights Movement eras brought tremendous developments in American drama. But by the mid-'70s, new conditions in the nation - political, social, cultural, and technological - combined to displace drama as a major vehicle of cultural expression (Herman 9). The move of drama from the center of the cultural stage has not meant its death, however. With Broadway's loss of primacy, regional, Off-, and Off-Off-Broadway activities have come to the fore, and this has meant unparalleled growth for minority (black, Chicano, women, gay) productions. In style and subject matter new patterns and concerns have arisen. Reverting to what Gerald M. Berkowitz defines as the mainstay of twentieth-century American drama, domestic realism, dramatists have started to express their concerns "through the everyday, personal experiences of ordinary characters" (167). In black drama, the traditional emphasis on cultural identity has continued. Instead of Amiri Baraka's once-dominant revolutionary style, characterized by images of revolt (Bigsby, Critical 414), at work now is the claim to possess an authentic black culture expressed through a recognizably black sensibility. This emphasis can be seen ...

Messengers of Culture : The Glory of African Beadwork.

© The World and I February 1, 2000
Outward appearance is the surest way to differentiate one person from another, and the desire for objects that can decorate or distinguish the individual appears to be universal. In fact, the practice of personal adornment is at least twenty-five thousand years old. Evidence found in Stone Age graves and domestic sites includes objects that are recognizable as jewelry. Ivory beads, necklaces made from fish vertebrae, and other objects are frequently uncovered in such locations.

Wearing distinctive apparel and adornments conveys specific personal and social information. Indeed, the physical expression of a culture is made as evident through ornament and dress as it is through ritual and ceremony. The form of decorative objects depends, of course, on the materials at hand. Historically, these were either local products or things acquired in trade. So it is with the beadwork of Africa. Beaded jewelry is a rich tradition in African culture but one with fairly recent origins. Curiously, it is a tradition dependent on imported European beads, trinkets brought to Africa as objects of trade.

Beads have become powerful elements in African life. Their use offers insight into hundreds of cultures. The jewelry worn by East Africa's Masai and Samburu people incorporates ...

ALL HAIL ATUNDA! POPULARITY AND ANARCHY IN THE MUSIC OF FELA ANIKULAPO KUTI

© Black Renaissance/Renaissance Noire July 1, 2003

If you could see Fela in the seventies - - the man turned Nigeria completely upside down! He had the whole country in his hand; it was as if he owned Nigeria! To tell the truth, Fela at that time was a law unto himself and did whatever he pleased in Nigeria, until he met an equally lawless group -- the army.

UNIDENTIFIED NIGERIAN FAN, Lagos, March 1992

It is being educated in the English way that makes you a big man (in Nigeria) That is what I disagree with. My message was: "Think African. Make students read African history" The people listened, but the government did not. That was when my confrontation with the government started. FELA ANIKULAPO KUTI (From Michael ...

Obasanjo, Nigeria and the World

© The International Journal of African Historical Studies January 1, 2012
Obasanjo, Nigeria and the World. By John Iliffe. Woodbridge, Suffolk: James Currey, 2011. Pp. xiii, 326; maps, bibliography, index. $80.00/£45.

Olusegun Obasanjo served as Nigeria's head of state on two separate occasions, as a military leader in the late-1970s and as an elected civilian president between 1999 and 2007. Obasanjo rose to prominence as one of the leading federal officers in the Biafran civil war, and his opposition to the Sani Abacha administration saw him imprisoned for three years in the 1990s. John Iliffe provides a comprehensive and engaging survey of Obasanjo's life and career from his birth in 1937 and humble origins to his retirement after 2007. The book is ...

Alain Ricard, The Languages and Literatures of Africa: the sands of Babel.(Book review)

© Africa September 22, 2007
ALAIN RICARD, The Languages and Literatures of Africa: the sands of Babel (translated by Naomi Morgan). Oxford: James Currey, Trenton NJ: Africa World Press and Cape Town: David Philip (pb 15.95-[pounds sterling] 0 85255 581 4). 2004, 230 pp.

The present book is the updated and expanded version of an earlier publication in French by Ricard, Litteratures d'Afrique noire: des langues aux livres (CNRS/Karthala, 1995). The new subtitle, 'the sands of Babel', borrowed from Chapter 9 and echoed in the book's closing remarks, aptly points to the multilingualism that characterizes the continent and has an impact on its literatures. The book's cover image is a photo of Soyinka, whose work is widely acknowledged as 'the crown jewel of Anglophone literature' (p. 180), ...

Sierra Leone

© Worldmark Encyclopedia of Religious Practices January 1, 2006

POPULATION 5,614,743
MUSLIM 60 percent
AFRICAN TRADITIONAL RELIGION 30 percent
CHRISTIAN 10 percent

Country Overview

INTRODUCTION
The Republic of Sierra Leone is a small West African country between Guinea and Liberia. Mountains in the east slope down to an upland plateau, wooded hills, and an Atlantic Coastal belt of mangrove swamps. About two-thirds of the inhabitants are subsistence farmers, but diamond mining provides the main hard currency. The Mende and Temne, the largest of the 18 principal ethnic groups, account for 60 percent of the population. Mende is spoken in the south, Temne in the north, and a literate minority speaks English (the official language). Ninety-five percent of the population also speak Krio, an English-based Creole.

Muslim traders and clerics brought Islam to northern Sierra Leone in the thirteenth century. Most Sierra Leonean Muslims are Sunnis, though some 10,000 Lebanese traders are Shiites. Portuguese explorers introduced Christianity on the mountainous, 25-mile-long Sierra Leone peninsula in 1462. Father Baltasar Barreira (1531–1612), a Catholic Jesuit priest, recommended that England and America settle freed slaves there. In 1787 a British Protestant abolitionist, Granville Sharp, established a settlement on the ...

Me and my shadow: a remarkable first novel from a young Brit haunts the mind and soul.(Helen Oyeyemi)(Critical Essay)

© Black Issues Book Review November 1, 2005

Can a writer step out of herself and write a novel? Helen Oyeyemi, author of the novel The Icarus Girl, says she did just that.

"The best part of The Icarus Girl was leaving myself behind and imagining, taking a diasporic look at Nigerian myth and this strong, brave, whimsical, precocious little girl that I wanted to get to know," Oyeyemi says.

Writers often talk about holding conversations with their characters. Some authors even wonder where their stories come from. But if the story isn't from the author, well, where is it from? Is it possible for a writer to be haunted? Of course, many believe that even the Bible was distorted by the messenger.

Confusing isn't it? It all really depends on what you want to believe. But that's the beauty of it. The same can be said about Oyeyemi's remarkable debut novel, The Icarus Girl.

In the novel, eight-year-old Jessamy Harrison, born to a Yoruba (Nigerian) mother and a white, British father, is a sharp-minded girl who spends much of her time reading Shakespeare and writing haiku. However, when life gets too demanding she has a habit of throwing screaming tantrums and being antisocial.

Twin Spirits

...

Genova, Ann

© Contemporary Authors January 1, 2008

PERSONAL:
Education: University of Texas at Austin, Ph.D., 2007.

ADDRESSES:
Office—Roanoke College, 9 North College 210, 221 College Ln., Salem, VA 24153. E-mail—genova@roanoke.edu.

CAREER:
Writer, editor, and educator. Roanoke College, Salem, VA, assistant professor of history.

WRITINGS:
(Editor, with Toyin Falola) *Yoruba Creativity: Fiction, Language, Life, and Songs,* Africa World Press (Trenton, NJ), 2004.

(Editor, with Toyin Falola) *Orisa: Yoruba Gods and Spiritual Identity in Africa and the Diaspora,* Africa World Press (Trenton NJ), 2005.

(With Toyin Falola) *The Politics of the Global Oil Industry: An Introduction,* Praeger (Westport, CT), 2005.

(Editor, with Toyin Falola) *Yoruba Identity and Power Politics,* University of Rochester Press (Rochester, NY), 2006.

(Editor, with Toyin Falola) *The Yoruba in Transition: History, Values, and Modernity,* Carolina Academic Press (Durham, NC), 2006.

SIDELIGHTS:
Ann Genova is a writer, historian, and educator based at Roanoke College in Salem, Virginia, where she serves as ...

Manipulating The Sacred: Yoruba Art, Ritual, and Resistance in Brazilian Candomble.(Book review)

© African Arts June 22, 2007
Manipulating The Sacred Yoruba Art, Ritual, and Resistance in Brazilian Candomble by Mikelle Smith Omari-Tunkara

Detroit: Wayne State University Press, 2005. 208 pp., 44 b/w and 36 color illustrations, glossaries, bibliography, index. $29.95 softcover.

In Manipulating the Sacred: Yoruba Art, Ritual, and Resistance in Brazilian Candomble, Mikelle Smith Omari-Tunkara imparts a wealth of information about Candomble Nago, the religion that has linked Yoruba-based practice in Bahia, Brazil, with Yoruba religion in West Africa since the eighteenth century. The author argues that Candomble Nago provides its predominantly Afro-Brazilian participants not only spiritual guidance, but attainable opportunities for mobility that are otherwise unavailable from their subaltern position in Brazilian society. Candomble Nago initiates face economic and other types of hardships within and outside the boundaries that physically indicate the sacred sphere. The privileging of African priorities, customs, and concepts that takes place in Candomble Nago, however, makes their religious experience distinct. At the same time that Candomble Nago is dynamic and changing, as evidenced by the gods, customs, and rituals that diverge from the ...

Deities of the Yoruba and Fon Religions

© World Eras January 1, 2004
Sources

Vodon. Vodon (known as Voodoo in the African Diaspora) is the most important religious tradition among the West African Fon. Although the independence of this religion from that of the Yoruba is discernible, the remarkable similarities of the two religions in terms of metaphysical structures, overlapping of deities, and the affinities in cults make it possible to discuss the Fon and Yoruba religions together. The Fon, who migrated from Togo to Benin in the seventeenth century, and the Yoruba, one of the three major ethnic groups of Nigeria, have the same ethnic and cultural origins even though their geographic dispersal has located them in different modern states.

Yoruba Religions. Because of their large numbers in West Africa and their wide dispersal through slavery in the Americas, the Yoruba are probably the best-known West African ethnic culture in the world. In Africa, Nigeria and the Republic of Benin have the largest concentration of Yoruba and Yoruba religions. In the Americas, Yoruba cultural influences are most apparent in Brazil, Cuba, Haiti, Jamaica, Trinidad, and Tobago, especially in the religions of the masses, including Vodon, Santéria, Camdomblé, and Macumba, and so forth. (In 1989, it was estimated that more than seventy million African and New World peoples ...

African Music: A Bibliographical Guide to the Traditional, Popular, Art, and Liturgical Musics of Sub-Saharan Africa.

© Notes September 1, 1994

John Gray, an indefatigable bibliographer of African and African-American expressive culture, has provided us with the first reasonably up-to-date map of a vast and widely scattered body of literature. Although his bibliographic guide to African music is largely unannotated, it is remarkably comprehensive. Gray focuses on Africa below the Sahara, covering publications in English, French, German, Italian, and Russian, and taking in a large body of journalistic writing on popular music. African Music contains 5,105 citations, organized into six main sections loosely identifiable as cultural history and the arts, ethnomusicology, traditional music, popular music, art music, and church music. Three appendixes focus on bibliographic and discographic reference works, archives and research centers, and recorded materials, including a list of record stores and mail-order companies in North America and Europe which stock recordings of African music. Four indexes--organized by ethnic group, subject, artist, and author--provide basic points of entry to the information.

The first two sections, which address the wider interdisciplinary context of African music studies, are--perhaps predictably--the least satisfying. ...

Vodou

© Melton's Encyclopedia of American Religions January 1, 2009
African Theological Archministry
    Afro-American Vodoun
    Church of Lukumi Babalu Aye
    Church of the Seven African Powers
    Religious Order of Witchcraft
    Voodoo Spiritual Temple

African Theological Archministry

c/o Oyotunji African Yoruba Village, PO Box 51, Sheldon, SC 29941

In December 1973 a group of blacks from Harlem received national news coverage for their establishment of a "vodou kingdom" in Beaufort County, South Carolina. This kingdom was called the sacred village of Oyotunji, and it was headed by one of the founders, Oba (King) Efuntola Oseijeman Adelabu Adefunmi I (1928–2005), born Walter Eugene King. King had abandoned the Baptist Church of his family during his teens and begun a search for the ancient gods of Africa. He traveled to Haiti in 1954 and discovered vodou. Early in 1955 he traveled to Europe and North Africa, and upon his return to the United States he founded the Order of Damballah Hwedo Ancestor Priests. In 1959 he traveled to Cuba and was initiated in the Orisha-Vodou African priesthood by Afro-Cubans at Matanzas, Cuba. The Order of Damballah was then superceded by the Shango Temple, and in 1960 King incorporated the African Theological Archministry. The Shango Temple was then renamed the Yoruba Temple.

In 1970 King Efuntola ...

Validation of the Edinburgh Postnatal Depression Scale as a screening tool for depression in late pregnancy among Nigerian women

© Journal of Psychosomatic Obstetrics and Gynecology December 1, 2006
Abstract

This study aimed to examine the validity of the Edinburgh Postnatal Depression Scale (EPDS) as a screening tool for depression in late pregnancy among Nigerian women. A total of 182 women in late pregnancy (32-36 weeks) completed either the English or the translated Yoruba language version of the EPDS and a proportion of them were then assessed for the presence of DSM-IV major and minor depressive disorders using the MINI International Neuropsychiatric Interview. A cut-off score of 10 on the EPDS was found to be the best for screening for both major and minor depression (sensitivity = 0.867, specificity = 0.915, Diagnostic Likelihood Ratio for a positive result= 10.200). ...

Voodoo

© Encyclopedia of American Religions January 1, 2003
★ 2011 ★

African Theological Archministry

% Oyotunji African Yoruba Village
Box 51
Sheldon, SC 29941

In December 1973 a group of blacks from Harlem received national news coverage for their establishment of a "voodoo kingdom" in Beaufort County, South Carolina. The sacred village of Oyotunji is headed by King Oba Efuntola Oseijeman Adelabu Adefunmi I, born Walter Eugene King in 1928. King abandoned the Baptist Church of his family during his teens and began a search for the ancient gods of Africa. He traveled to Haiti in 1954 and discovered voodoo. Early in 1955, he travelled to Europe and North Africa and upon his return to the United States, he founded the Order of Damballah Hwedo Ancestor Priests. Then in 1959, he traveled to Cuba and was initiated in the Orisha-Vodu African priesthood by Afro-Cubans at Matanzas, Cuba. The Order of Damballah was superceded by the Shango Temple and in 1960 he incorporated the African Theological Archministry. The Shango Temple was renamed the Yoruba Temple.

In 1970 King Efuntola, as King became known, moved with most of the temple members to rural South Carolina where the Yoruba Village of Oyotunji was established. He began a complete reform of the Orisha-Vodu priesthood along Nigerian lines. In 1972 he traveled to Nigeria and was initiated ...

The Yoruba Diaspora in the Atlantic World

© Ibero-americana July 1, 2005
Toyin Falola and Matt D. Childs, [eds.], The Yoruba Diaspora in the Atlantic World. Bloomington and Indianapolis: Indiana University Press, 2004.

Although a marginalized field, the African Diaspora has been studied for about a century. In this volume, scholars from North and South America, Africa and Europe discuss historical and ongoing changes and innovations in African and American Yoruba communities. The theoretical perspective, presented in chapter one, calls for the scholarly inclusion of communities on both sides of the Atlantic in order to understand the African Diaspora, and in response to this call, the nineteen essays focus on a diverse set of aspects of the Yoruba ...

Various: Havana, Cuba, Ca. 1957: Rhythms And Songs For The Orishas & Matanzas, Cuba, Ca. 1957: Afro-Cuban Sacred Music From The Countryside.

© Sing Out! March 22, 2002
VARIOUS Havana, Cuba, CA. 1957: Rhythms And Songs For The Orishas Smithsonian/Folkways 40489

VARIOUS Matanzas, Cuba, CA. 1957: Afro-Cuban Sacred Music From The Countryside Smithsonian/Folkways 40490

These recordings are gleaned from the work of Cuban ethnographer Lydia Cabrera and photographer Josephena Tarafa when they added sound recordings to their urban and rural fieldwork. Like a musical genome, these recordings serve as keys to the complex historical connections between West Africa, the Caribbean, and parts of South America. Attentive listening and a close read of the liner notes to Havana take you into the oru de igbodu, a cycle of bata (drum) salutes ...

Santísimo.(TT: Most Holy)

© Latin Beat Magazine February 1, 1997
Led by Emilio Barreto, Priest of Obatala in the Santeria religion, Santisimo pays homage to the African deities of the Yoruba religion. From the millions of African people brought by slave traders to the Americas in the 19th century, the Yoruba of Nigeria evoked within themselves a rich religious system in Cuba that evolved into what is known as "Santeria." The Yoruba in Cuba preserved these sacred traditions in secret for many years as well as did the Yoruba in Brazil where the religion is called Condomble, in Trinidad where it known as Shango, and in Haiti where it is called Vodun. The Yoruba religion is based on one God, Olodumare, and the deified forces of nature known as ...

Up and coming in Las Vegas: el Rumband de Miguel Zamarripa. (música latina jazz)(TT: Up and coming in Las Vegas: the Rumband of Miguel Zamarripa)

(TA: Latin jazz music)
© Latin Beat Magazine December 1, 1997
El Rumband de Miguel Zamarripa

Las Vegas, Nevada may be in a desert and synonymous with neon lights and slot machines, but culturally it is not barren. With the accelerated growth in population that has been taking place for the last decade, the arts are also enjoying great interest, as the influx of artists and musicians continues. One of these musicians is a Canadian-born musician by the name of Miguel Zamarripa, of Mexican and Canadian extraction. Miguel migrated to Las Vegas where he met his pianist wife, Brigitte LeClerc. Both are members of the orchestra of Cirque Du Soleil and Mystere, now appearing at the Treasure Island Hotel and Casino.

He began playing ...

Recurrent themes in the poetry of Yoruba female writers. (Report)

© Journal of Pan African Studies August 1, 2007
Introduction

Toril Moi noted that as early as 1971 Elaine Showalter (as quoted by Register: 1975) called on critics to examine the works of female writers in order to have a deep knowledge of their arts (p. 50). Also, there is a need to re-enfranchise women writers into the mainstream of academic curriculum through a fairer, non-sex biased, and more judicious appraisals of their work. This is what this paper intends to achieve as it examines the themes of Yoruba poems written by women and contend that the poems are essentially socio-political commentary which at the time of publication, pre-occupied Yoruba society, and Nigeria at large.

Taking a broad look at Yoruba studies in general, few women are featured among writers in Yoruba language, and most especially in poetic writings. Nevertheless, this does not mean there are no thriving creative activities going on among Yoruba women (many reasons may be adduced to this lacking). First, it may be due to the pre-occupation of womenfolk with domestic affairs. And secondly, the observation of Stimpson in Benstock (1987) has captured some of the rationale behind this when she says:

... men have controlled history, politics, and culture. They have decided who will have power and ...

THE USE OF HUMAN IMAGES IN YORUBA MEDICINES(1).

© Ethnology June 22, 2000
Indigenous healers among the Yoruba of southwestern Nigeria regularly utilize small carved and molded three-dimensional human figures in their medicines. These figures are used by individuals in purposeful acts of magical mimesis to manipulate the social world. Four major types of Yoruba medicine figures act as surrogates, messengers, and the Yoruba everyman/woman to activate forces affecting individual lives. (Nigeria, Yoruba, medicine, art, magic)

The centrality of the human body to cultural thought makes it a powerful mimetic referent that "mediates all reflection and action upon the world" (Lock 1993). This is clearly seen in indigenous medical systems throughout the world where the unseeable powers of nature are anthropomorphized in the form of two- and three-dimensional human figures used as ingredients in magical medicines, charms, and amulets.(2) Usually discussed in terms of sympathetic magic, the figures act to direct or store these powers for a variety of positive and negative purposes. In replication of the human form as artifact, supernatural powers are encapsulated and controlled to be brought into the cultural realm where they can be manipulated to benefit individuals or groups.

In the tradition described here, the Yoruba of southwestern Nigeria carve and mold ...

A MALE-CENTRIC MODIFICATION OF HISTORY: EFUNSETAN ANIWURA REVISITED

© History In Africa January 1, 2004
I

Historical drama can be described as a form of drama which purports to reflect or represent historical proceedings. Since time immemorial writers have combined fiction and history in creative works. Lawrence Langner has ascribed the popularity of historical drama to the desire of the theatergoer to spend an evening in the company of kings, queens, and other historical personages; the opportunity to become familiar with far greater events than those which take place in the lives of ordinary people; and that historical plays recreate great deeds done by great personages in the past.1 Historical facts are then creatively adapted and made available in play form to the audience. ...

Pet-naming as protest's discourse in polygamous Yoruba homes: a socio-pragmatic study.(Report)

© Studies in Literature and Language February 29, 2012
INTRODUCTION

The patriarchal system of authority in Africa has influenced a lot of other socio-cultural phenomena including marriage. Thus, the male chauvinist is allowed to have more than one woman as his legal wives. These women (who are not happy at the turn of events in their matrimonial homes) are always at loggerheads with one another and with their husbands. In a bid to protest and retaliate, each woman buys one pet and exercises her (naming) power over the latter by giving it a symbolic name. Psychologically, these names are meant to mitigate the suffering and punishment that each of the participants is passing through in such a polygamous setting; socially, they serve as instruments of protest but pragmatically, they perform different illocutionary functions in the contexts. This study considers twenty pet names as used in polygamous Yoruba setting(s), with a view to underscoring their speech act functions.
THE YORUBA GROUP

The Yoruba numbered about five million people inhabiting the South western part of Nigeria. They are a major group of people with common language, cultural heritage and geographical boundary. They predominantly occupy six states (Ekiti, Lagos, Ogun, Osun, Ondo and ...

Worldview, the Orichas, and Santería: Africa to Cuba and Beyond

© The International Journal of African Historical Studies January 1, 2007
Worldview, the Orichas, and Santería: Africa to Cuba and Beyond. By Mercedes Cros Sandoval. Gainesville: University Press of Florida, 2006. Pp. xxvi, 416, 19 illustrations. $59.95.

Sandoval's ambitious new work attempts to provide a broad overview of the overlapping spaces shared by Yoruba traditional religion and the Diaspora's Santería. Her emphasis on worldview, a concept that is resuscitated for this project, tries to bridge the gap between the worlds, waters, and cultures that feed into the international nature of orisha world religions by looking at very broad cultural perspectives. Part memoir, part encyclopedia, part ethnography - this volume reads like many different ...

African Caribbean Slave Mothers and Children: Traumas of Dislocation and Enslavement Across the Atlantic World

© Caribbean Quarterly March 1, 2010
Early European accounts of the West Coast of Africa provided representations of the fecundity of women and the high value placed on motherhood. African mothers were central to transmitting family memory and the culture and values of their communities and enslaved women carried this knowledge through to the plantation. Mother Africa is evoked by Yemoja, an Orisha of the Yoruba religion, the essence of motherhood and the protector of children, and other similar deities relating to female fertility who travelled with Africans across the Atlantic. The historian, Basil Davidson, used the term 'Black Mother' to evoke Africa as a source of enslaved people and Mother Poem by the Caribbean poet, ...

Assessing elemental mercury

vapor exposure from cultural and religious practices.

© Environmental Health Perspectives August 1, 2001

Use of elemental mercury in certain cultural and religious practices can cause high exposures to mercury vapor. Uses include sprinkling mercury on the floor of a home or car, burning it in a candle, and mixing it with perfume. Some uses can produce indoor air mercury concentrations one or two orders of magnitude above occupational exposure limits. Exposures resulting from other uses, such as infrequent use of a small bead of mercury, could be well below currently recognized risk levels. Metallic mercury is available at almost all of the 15 botanicas visited in New York, New Jersey, and Pennsylvania, but botanica personnel often deny having mercury for sale when approached by outsiders to these religious and cultural traditions. Actions by public health authorities have driven the mercury trade underground in some locations. Interviews indicate that mercury users are aware that mercury is hazardous, but are not aware of the inhalation exposure risk. We argue against a crackdown by health authorities because it could drive the practices further underground, because high-risk practices may be rare, and because uninformed government intervention could have unfortunate political and civic side effects for some Caribbean and Latin American ...

The African Diaspora: A History Through Culture

© The International Journal of African Historical Studies January 1, 2011
The African Diaspora: A History Through Culture. By Patrick Manning. Columbia Studies in Global and International History. New York: Columbia University Press, 2009. Pp. ix-xxi, 395; maps, graphs and tables, photographs, illustrations, notes, index. $24.50 / £17 paper.

Patrick Manning's The African Diaspora: A History Through Culture is an ambitious and far-reaching volume that puts Africa and the African Diaspora at the center of world history. Like Michael Gomez in Reversing Sail: A History of the African Diaspora (Cambridge University Press, 2005), John Thornton and Linda Heywood in Central Africans, Atlantic Creoles, and the Foundation of the Americas, 1585-1660 (Cambridge ...

Gary Stroutsos Oru: The Natural Order.(Sound Recording Review)

© Sing Out! January 1, 2003
Paras 1123

In his latest offering, Native style flutist Gary Stroutsos has looked for inspiration to the liturgy of the Yoruba religion, as practiced in the nation of Cuba. He has transposed the melodies of worship, of elemental invocation, to the muted crispness of the Native flute. Despite backup by Cuban musicians culled by the CD's producer Danilo Lozano, Stroutsos creates music that is still searching for roots.

Imagine "Ave Maria" on the accordion; the "Hallelujah Chorus" on sitar. The limitations of the instruments demand their music be executed in a certain way. So, too, with Native flute. Stroutsos has chosen the Orisa songs, melodies of praise and ...

Militant Legacy

© Michigan Quarterly Review May 6, 2000 Riott, Eddie
Michigan Citizen
05-06-2000
Militant Legacy

Never has been a mode militant musician than Fela Kuti. Not Paul Robeson, not Bob Marley, certainly no Chuck D. No one exceeds the rancorous fire of the late African superstar. He used his music as a sword - stabbing at the heart of racism, colonialism, corruption, police brutality, and corporate mind control.

Fela's group - Nigeria '70, Africa '70 and finally Egypt '80 - became his pulpit of perching African emancipation and pan-African unity, while chastising African dictators. In the process he recorded more than 50 albums, most of which were only briefly available as discs in the ...

Resources for teaching "women and religion": five readers. (Book Reviews).(Book Review)

© Feminist Collections: A Quarterly of Women's Studies Resources January 1, 2003
Elizabeth A. Castelli, ed., with Rosamond C. Rodman, WOMEN, GENDER, RELIGION: A READER. New York: Palgrave, 2001. 550p. bibl. $89.95, ISBN 0-312-24004-X; pap., $27.95, ISBN 0-312-24030-9.

Nancy Auer Falk & Rita M. Gross, eds., UNSPOKEN WORLDS: WOMEN'S RELIGIOUS LIVES. Belmont, CA: Wadsworth, 2000 (3rd ed). 310p. bibl. ill, pap., $43.95, ISBN 0-534-51570-3.

Darlene M. Juschka, ed., FEMINISM IN THE STUDY OF RELIGION: A READER. London & New York: Continuum, 2000 (cloth), 2001 (pap.). 693p. bibl. index. $107.95, ISBN 08264-4726-0; pap., $29.95, ISBN 0-8264-4727-9.

Nancy Nason-Clark & Mary Jo Neitz, eds., FEMINIST NARJMTIVES AND THE SOCIOLOGY OF RELIGION Walnut Creek, CA: AltaMira, 2001. 141p. bibl. $59.00, ISBN 0-7591-0197-3; pap., $19.95, ISBN 0-7591-0198-1.

Lucinda Joy Peach, WOMEN AND WORLD RELIGIONS. Upper Saddle River, NJ: Prentice Hall, 2002. 394p. bibl. index, pap., $36.20, ISBN 0-13-040444-6.

In preparing to write this essay, I surveyed a number of syllabi for undergraduate courses in "Women and Religion" from a variety of colleges and universities. I wanted to see how others teaching these courses understand the subject and what ...

West Indian Rhythm: Trinidad Calypsos on World and Local Events, Featuring the Censored Recordings 1938-1940

© Folk Music Journal January 1, 2008
West Indian Rhythm: Trinidad Calypsos on World and Local Events, Featuring the Censored Recordings 1938-

1940 Edited by the Classic Calypso Collective. Notes by John H. Cowley, Donald R. Hill, Hollis Liverpool, Denis Malins-Smith, Richard Noblett, Dick Spottswood, and Lise Winer. Boxed set of 10 CDs with book. 316 pp. Illus. Discog. Bear Family Records BCD 16623 JM, 2006.

During the past few years, there have been numerous reissues of historical calypso recordings, including more than a dozen CDs from Rounder Records. This ten-CD box from Bear Family addresses itself to the same audience of collectors and calypso fans. However, it is not just another well-produced reissue. The ...

Letters

© New African May 1, 2008
China-Africa: Why the West is worried

Thanks for you article on the relations between China and Africa (New African, March 2008). Like you correctly pointed out, the relations between these two great peoples date back to centuries ago. China has strived so hard and so ably to treat Africa with understanding and equality. When Margaret Thatcher and Ronald Reagan turned their backs on us in exchange for Kruger gold coins with racist South Africa in their so-called "constructive engagement" policy, China stood with the oppressed people of Africa and gave them refuge, solace and material support. When presidents Kenneth Kaunda of Zambia and Mwalimu Julius Nyerere of Tanzania courted ...

The African Difference: Discourses on Africanity and the Relativity of Cultures.

© Journal of Asian and African Studies December 1, 1997
Oyekan Owomoyela, (New York: Peter Lang, 1996), xii, 236 pp. Paper, no price reported.

This book is a clarion call for other Africanists to join the battle for Africa (and Africanity), which the author argues is in a new and more difficult era than during colonialism, when the lines were clearly drawn and the choices were simple. Divided into nine chapters, this book covers themes such as language, identity and social construction, philosophy, ideology, culture, technology, the New World Order, gender, myths and mystification, epistemology and methodology, and America in African imagination and literature. Some of the essays in this book were originally presented at scholarly fora over the years; the others have previously ...

The Study of Religions in Africa: Past, Present and Prospects.

© Africa March 22, 1998
JAN PLATVOET, JAMES COX and JACOB OLUPONA (eds), The Study of Religions in Africa: past, present and prospects. Cambridge: Roots & Branches, 1996, 393 pp., SEK 282, ISBN 0 9525772 2 4.

This book consists of the proceedings of a conference of the International Association for the History of Religions (IAHR) which took place in Harare, Zimbabwe, in 1992, the first to be held on the African continent. It is also the first volume in a new series of publications sponsored by the African Association for the Study of Religions co-edited by Jacob Olupona and David Westerlund. The book is a self-conscious attempt to mark these events as reflecting a transition in the academic study of religion in Africa, and many of the seventeen contributions were written with the intention of taking stock of the present state of this academic discipline on the African continent and of opening up debate about certain conceptual and methodological issues.

There is a refreshingly `ecumenical' tone to this collection of articles, best exemplified perhaps by Jan G. ...

Agenda.(Calendar)

© New York March 3, 2008
1 THE CLASSIC

Perhaps you never expected to see Aphra Behn's 1688 slave novella Oroonoko outside of a Norton Anthology--but the Theatre for a New Audience production is very much alive, thanks to vibrant Yoruba music and dance and a revelatory performance by Albert Jones as the enslaved prince torn between love and revenge. Through March 9.
[ILLUSTRATION OMITTED]
2 THE IMAGE

After a chance encounter in 2002, Muzi Quawson spent four years photographing Amanda Jo Williams, a rangy down-and-out rocker and mother living upstate in Woodstock. The twelve photographs displayed in "Pull Back the Shade"--Quawson's first solo show in the States--are gritty and luminous, spare portraits of an artist working far outside the glamour and cash nexus of the art world. Through March 29 at Yossi Milo.
[ILLUSTRATION OMITTED]
3 THE NEW WAVE

Fifty-eight teenage girls wrote essays for Red (the Book), an anthology of authentic young voices at their most raw and witty. (All 58 blog at redthebook. com.) Nine New York contributors will read essays covering eternal adolescent topics, from gym class to converting out of your parents' religion to "Jewish hair." February 28 at the Lower East Side Tenement Museum.
[ILLUSTRATION OMITTED]
4 THE SENTENCE ...

Ward, Ida Caroline (1880–1949)

© Women in World History: A Biographical Encyclopedia January 1, 2002
British phonetician and West African language scholar . Born on October 4, 1880, in Bradford, Yorkshire, England; died on October 10, 1949, in Guildford, England; daughter of Samson Ward (a wool merchant) and Hannah (Tempest) Ward; educated in Bradford and at the Darlington Training College; Durham University, B.Litt., 1902; London University, Ph.D., 1933; never married.

Born in 1880 in Yorkshire, England, Ida Caroline Ward was the eighth child of Samson and Hannah Ward , and received her early education in her hometown of Bradford. After attending the Darlington Training College, she went on to graduate from Durham ...

Afro-Cuban Religions

© Contemporary American Religion January 1, 1999
In Cuba, the largest Caribbean island,

African religions were introduced by slaves coming from West and Central Africa. Santería is the most famous of Afro-Cuban religions, but it is not the only one. At least three other Afro-Cuban religious traditions can be identified: the cult of Ifá, the Palo Monte, and Cuban Spiritualism. These religions evolved in colonial and postcolonial Cuban society. They influenced one another and were influenced by Spanish Catholicism. They also had contacts with Spiritualism, which penetrated Cuba in the second part of the nineteenth century. It is important to note that these four traditions are not exclusive and that the practitioners still consider themselves as Catholics in Cuba. After Fidel Castro came to power in 1959, some believers left the country and settled in the United States, especially in Florida and around New York, where they continued practicing these four main Afro-Cuban religions.

One Afro-Cuban tradition is ...

Baraka, Amiri

© Contemporary Poets January 1, 2001
Nationality: African-American. Born: Everett LeRoi Jones in Newark, New Jersey, 7 October 1934; took name Amiri Baraka in 1968. Education: Attended Central Avenue School and Barringer High School, Newark; Rutgers University, Newark, New Jersey, 1951–52; Howard University, Washington, D.C., 1953–54. Military Service: U.S. Air Force, 1954–57. Family: Married 1) Hettie Roberta Cohen in 1958 (divorced 1965), two daughters; 2) Sylvia Robinson (now Amina Baraka) in 1967, five children; also two stepdaughters and two other daughters. Career: Teacher, New School for Social Research, New York, 1961–64, and Summers, 1977–79, State University of New York, Buffalo, Summer 1964, and Columbia University, New York, 1964 and Spring 1980; visiting professor, San Francisco State College, 1966–67, Yale University, New Haven, Connecticut, 1977–78, and George Washington University, Washington, D.C., 1978–79. Assistant professor, 1980–82, associate professor, 1983–84, professor of Africana Studies, 1985–96, and since 1996 professor emeritus, State University of New York, Stony Brook. Founder, *Yugen* magazine and Totem Press, New York, 1958–62; editor, with Diane di Prima, *Floating Bear* magazine, New York, 1961–63; founding director, Black Arts Repertory Theatre, Harlem, New York, 1964–66; founding director, ...

Peterson, Nancy J. 1958-

© Contemporary Authors January 1, 2004
PERSONAL: Born March 4, 1958 in Minneapolis, MN. *Education:* University of Wisconsin—Madison, B.A., 1980, Ph.D., 1991; University of North Texas, M.A., 1985.

ADDRESSES: Office—Department of English, Purdue University, 500 Oval Drive, West Lafayette, IN 47907-2038. *E-mail*—njp@purdue.edu.

CAREER: Educator and writer. Purdue University, West Lafayette, IN, associate professor of English. *Modern Fiction Studies,* associate editor.

MEMBER: Modern Language Association, American Studies Association.

WRITINGS:

(Editor) *Toni Morrison: Critical and Theoretical Approaches,* Johns Hopkins University Press (Baltimore, MD), 1997.

Against Amnesia: Contemporary Women Writers and the Crises of Historical Memory, University of Pennsylvania Press (Philadelphia, PA), 2001.

Contributor to *The Chippewa Landscape of Louise Erdrich,* edited by Allan Chavkin, University of Alabama Press (Tuscaloosa, AL), 1994; and *Productive Post-modernism: Consuming Histories and* ...

Santería

© Encyclopedia of African-American Culture and History January 1, 2006
Santería, or "saint worship," is a religion that has its roots in both the spiritual practices of the Yoruba people of western Africa and in Roman Catholicism. The Yoruba people believed in the supreme God Olodumare and in lesser deities known as *orishas*. As slaves brought to work on sugar plantations in Cuba, they were baptized and catechized in the Roman Catholic Church in accordance with the Slave Code of 1789. The synthesis of these two religious practices occurred as slaves began to recognize Catholic saints as spiritual beings similar to their *orishas*. Eventually each *orisha* was matched with a Catholic saint and came to be ...

Profile: New Orleans hosts jazz festival

© NPR Tavis Smiley May 3, 2004
TAVIS SMILEY
Tavis Smiley (NPR)
05-03-2004
Profile: New Orleans hosts jazz festival

Host: TAVIS SMILEY
Time: 9:00-10:00 AM

TAVIS SMILEY, host:

New Orleans this weekend concluded its annual Jazz & Heritage Festival. Writer Askia Mohammed was in the Crescent City for the celebration. He shares with us some of his memories of gumbo, Po-Boys and jambalaya.

ASKIA MOHAMMED reporting:

Outside of southern Louisiana, New Orleans may be best known for its annual Mardi Gras bacchanal or as a favorite Super Bowl or convention venue. But here in the Big Easy itself, the New Orleans Jazz & Heritage Festival is no secret. It is the best party ...

Collaboration abroad for women scientists. (International). (Women's International Science Collaboration program)(Brief Article)

© Science May 31, 2002
By day, the tank drove Lyn Gualtieri and her Russian research partner through the Siberian forest, as they looked for rocks left behind by ancient glaciers. By night, it provided refuge

from bears. Doing research from an armored vehicle was "pretty surreal," recalled Gualtieri, a postdoctoral researcher at the University of Washington, whose trip was made possible by a grant from WISC--AAAS's Women's International Science Collaboration program.

Launched in 2001, the WISC program aims to increase the participation of women in international scientific research. The program is administered by AAAS and funded by the National Science Foundation (NSF). It provides women scientists ...

Chucho Valdés 99.(pianista; conducta de vida)(TT: Chucho Valdés 99.)(TA: pianist; conduct of life)

© Latin Beat Magazine June 1, 1999
In Cuba the surname Valdés is common. When it was mentioned in Cuba during the '50s, two musicians came to mind, Vicentico Valdés or Bebo Valdés, the two most popular Valdés in Cuba at the time. Today, not only in Cuba, but wherever the sound of jazz has been heard, the mere mention of Valdés mentally produces the race of Jesús "Chucho" Valdés, the brilliant pianist and musical director of Cuba's Grupo Irakere. In 1978, Americans became aware of Chucho via his Columbia label recording of Irakere Live, recorded at Carnegie Hall. It won a Grammy in the Tropical Music category in 1979.

Twelve years later, during March, 1991, Michael Greene, Chairman of the Grammy Awards organization travelled to Havana to present the Grammy to Chucho. In a simple ceremony at the International Conference Center, Chucho thanked the sponsors of the award for having honored Irakere's ...

Jose Mangual Jr. Dancing With the Gods.(Reseña de audio grabación)

© Latin Beat Magazine February 1, 2004
(Chola Musical Productions)
Master percussionist José Mangual Jr. pays homage to the deities of the Yoruba religion through salsa beat interpretations. Opening with the selection Tumbayaya, Mangual salutes palo mayombe, the Congo-derived religion that predates many of the Yoruba beliefs. He then proceeds with the traditional invocation of Elegguá, his arrangement of the Sonora Matancera's classic hit Saludo a Elegguá. The dancing homage to the Yoruba gods continues throughout the eleven hardcore salsa tracks of this new production. This excellent, joyful "bembé" ...

Book explores religions and the significance of difference.(God is not One: The Eight Rival Religions that Run the World)(Book review)

© National Catholic Reporter September 16, 2011
In a world rife with religious conflict and militant fundamentalism, the temptation is strong to emphasize the unity of religions. On one side, those hostile to religion will blame all religions for similarly perpetuating ignorance and violence. For these people, the world would be a safer place without religion. On the other side, those eager to promote interreligious harmony will argue that religions are really different paths up the same mountain. For these people, the world would be a safer place if only people could understand that, basically, all religions are saying the same thing.

According to aiepnen rromero, a proiessor 01 religion at Boston University who has appeared everywhere from CNN to "The Colbert Report," both sides are wrong. Even as adherents of religious traditions are party to some of the most egregious violations of human dignity, they are also behind some of the most powerful movements for peace and justice. Moreover, he contends, religious ...

Odunde African Street Festival.

© American Visions June 1, 2000
Odunde African Street Festival
WHERE: African Market Square, Philadelphia (215) 732-8508 http://www.odunde.org
WHEN: June 11
WHAT: A celebration of odunde, a Yoruba word meaning "Happy New Year"
WHY: To mark the coming of another year for African Americans and Africanized people around the world

Each year, hundreds of people attend Philadelphia's African Street Festival, which focuses on the cultural enrichment of the African-American community. The festival begins with a colorful procession to the Schuykill River, where offerings of fruits and flowers are made to Oshun, the goddess of the river. During the procession, praise is ...

Africanity vs Blackness: Race, class and culture in Brazil

© NACLA Report on the Americas May 1, 2002
REPORT ON RACE AND IDENTITY
Most of what the world knows as Brazilian culture, and what Brazil projects in international performance, is of African origin. When one thinks of the music and dance of the country, the image that usually comes to mind is the compelling rhythms and intricate footwork and hip movements of samba, and the excitement of carnival. European pre-Catholic "pagan" in origin, carnival acquired its reputation as the world's biggest party as a result of the masquerading and parading traditions of Africans and their descendants, who in Brazil and elsewhere in the Americas appropriated the celebration from the white elites who had prohibited them from participating, ...

Afro-Cuban Bata Rhythms: Part 1: History And Feel

© Modern Drummer : MD January 1, 2008
Afro-Cuban bata drums are known around the world as one of the most rhythmically complete instruments. These days, you can hear them in many popular genres. From hip-hop and jazz, to pop and salsa, the bata drums-which were once banned-are becoming an important component in the development of contemporary music.

Bata have an immense and rich vocabulary, so it's a great benefit for all drumset players to study the instrument's traditional rhythms. Learning bata will not only make it easier for you to perform other Afro-Cuban styles and world rhythms with the proper feel, it will also expand your rhythmic and melodic abilities in more conventional settings.

The traditional …

Cuba and the Tempest: Literature and Cinema in the Time of Diaspora

© The Hispanic Outlook in Higher Education April 7, 2008
By Humberto López Cruz

Cuba and the Tempest: Literature and Cinema in the Time of Diaspora, by Eduardo Gonzalez. 264 pages. Chapel Hill, N.C.: The University of North Carolina Press, 2006. ISBN 978-0-8078-5683-3. $24.95 paper.

The development of the seventh art continues in crescendo. The cinematographic industry exposes, with relative fidelity, everyday events as well as important international issues that somehow find their way into the imaginations of renowned contemporary novelists and fill the pages of their current projects. When we as readers find that a literature professor who is also a well-known cineaste carries out a study on the fusion of possible aspects from …

Distance Learning And Oral Traditions of Music: - A Case of Yoruba Drumming

© Indian Musicological Society. Journal of the Indian Musicological Society January 1, 2002

Distance learning, as I understand it, implies a lack of physical contact between the teacher and the learner. If this is the case, it appears that distance learning is not conducive to the mastery of oral traditions of Music.

One of the main points about orality as a technique of music education is that pupil and teacher are physically present in the same place. If this is a valid statement the implication is that the less a music tradition depends on orality for the acquisition of musical knowledge, the more susceptible it is to distance learning. Western art music, for example, is not generally regarded as an oral tradition and is therefore presumbly teachable through the …

The Mandala Project.(school art project)

© School Arts May 1, 1996

I teach art at the Essex Campus Program (ECP), an alternative high school for at-risk students. After receiving an "Arts for EveryKid Minigrant," I planned a series of events, including trips, guest speakers and lessons based on the concept of the mandala. The goals were to introduce mandalas and other geometric patterns of spiritual and artistic significance; to include the development of an inter-disciplinary curriculum; to introduce the geometry of circular design generation (math); to understand the mandala as a way to organize thought (creative writing); to learn how to make mandalas and what they mean in different cultures.

The Significance of the Mandala

Our first trip was to the Newark Museum where Curator of Asian Art Valrae Reynolds gave us a tour of the collections of Tibetan art and Nepalese mandalas. We looked at a mandala made of jewels and precious metals, created by a wealthy person as an offering. Reynolds spoke about the parts of the mandala …

Vocal Baobab: Yoruba Dream. (Sound Recording Review)

© Sing Out! March 22, 2006
VOCAL BAOBAB Yoruba Dream ARC Music 1966

Vocal Baobab are a young Havana-based folklore group. Their aim is to promote traditional Afro-Cuban music through the combination of the old and the contemporary. This, their first release, is an exploration of Santeria cantos and toques, the sounds that accompany the rituals and practices of the ancient Yoruba religion.

I find it difficult to understand the intention or, indeed, the purpose of this album. It is meant to be an illustration of a cult music. Therefore, it is grossly out of context in this form. Religious music, at the best of times, has limited mass appeal, and does not always readily make for …

Market Supply Response of Cassava Farmers in Ile-Ife, Osun State

© Canadian Social Science May 1, 2012
Abstract

This study examined the market supply response of cassava farmers in Ile-Ife, Osun State. Data were collected from 80 cassava farmers from four cassava producing Local Government Areas (LGAs) namely; Ife-East, Ife-Central, Ife-North and Ife-South. These were analysed using descriptive statistics and regression technique. The results of the descriptive analysis showed that method of cassava farming was mainly traditional and cassava was mostlly cultivated with maize. Majority of the cassava farmers were married, literate and of about 35 years meaning that more young people were into cassava cultivation in Ile-Ife. Also, the farmers had an average of 8 members per …

Yoruba Sacred Kingship: "A Power Like That of the Gods"

© Anthropological Quarterly July 1, 1998

Yoruba Sacred Kingship: "A Power Like That of the Gods." JOHN PEMBERTON III and FUNSO S. AFQLAYAN. Washington DC: Smithsonian Institution Press, 1996; 252 pp.

Yoruba sacred kingship is a vivid and detailed account of contemporary ritual life in the town of Ila, southwestern Nigeria. It focuses particularly on the annual cycle of rites for ancestors and gods (dri,sd) that undergirds the authority of the town's king, known as the Orangun, but it also attends to the rites that dramatize the historical autonomy of local sub-groups that have resisted the sovereignty of this king. In this setting the authors illuminate the interplay of dominant and subaltern histories while examining …

Varieties of African American Religious Experience

© Interpretation October 1, 1999

Varieties of African American Religious Experience, by Anthony B. Pinn. Fortress, Minneapolis, 1998. 242 pp. $17.00. ISBN 0-8006-29949.

AFRICAN AMERICAN THEOLOGY suffers from too narrow a canon of resources. Along with Christianity, suggests Pinn, a more holistic discussion of black religious experience should include other significant religious expressions. In four chapters he outlines Voodoo, Yoruba religion, Islam (and the Nation of Islam), and humanism (with a slight discussion of Black Unitarians). The enslavement of Africans is the starting point for Pinn's analysis of each religious expression. The central thesis of the text is that these other religious expressions have ...

Mali salvages African pride as Nigeria disappoints

© New African June 1, 1999

Osasu Obayiuwana, just back from the World Youth Championship in Nigeria, is full of praise for Mali, but for Nigeria (his motherland)... he is not so sure.

There are three religions that evoke indescribable passion in Africa's most populous country -- Christianity, Islam and football.

For Nigeria's estimated 120 million people and 300 ethnic groups, football is the much needed opium that provides a brief and often pleasurable escape from the harsh economic realities that have made daily life a bitter struggle for survival.

It is an ironic reflection of the Nigerian psyche that its people are calmly resigned to the deterioration of their once high living standards ...

Review: Orishas' debut "A Lo Cubano"

© NPR All Things Considered March 1, 2001 00-00-0000

Review: Orishas' debut "A Lo Cubano"
Host: ROBERT SIEGEL Time: 8:00-9:00 PM

ROBERT SIEGEL, host:
When the Buena Vista Social Club won a Grammy Award in 1998, it captured US attention. A series of celebrated spinoffs by the old guard of Cuban music followed. But in Cuba, the current favorites include many younger musicians, like a new hip-hop quartet called Orishas. The group is based, but they insist not exiled, in France. Banning Eyre has this review of Orishas' debut "A Lo Cubano."

BANNING EYRE reporting:
Orishas are deities in the Yoruba religion, which comes from Nigeria but survives, like so many ...

Death and the King's Horseman

© World Literature and Its Times: Profiles of Notable Literary Works and the Historic Events That Influenced Them January 1, 2000
by Wole Soyinka

THE LITERARY WORK
A play set in Oyo, the capital of the colonized Oyo kingdom in Nigeria, during World War II; published in English in 1975.

SYNOPSIS
Tragedy results from the failure of a traditional chief, Elesin Oba, the Master of the King's Stables, to commit ritual suicide on the last day of the funeral rites of his king, the Alaafin of Oyo.

Events in History at the Time the Play Takes Place
The *Play in Focus*
Events in History at the Time the Play Was Written
For More Information
Wole Soyinka, one of the best-known playwrights in the English-speaking world, was born in Abeokuta, Ogun State, Nigeria, in 1934. He attended St. Peter's School in Abeokuta, where his literary-minded father was the headmaster. At the prestigious Government College, a high school in Ibadan, Soyinka nurtured his literary interests by participating in the school's artistic and cultural activities and by reading extensively in the school's library. After high school Soyinka studied English at the University of Ibadan, and drama and theater at Leeds University in England. He went on to write and produce more than 20 plays, several films, two novels, three ...

Baraka, Amiri 1934-

© Contemporary Authors, New Revision Series January 1, 2005
(LeRoi Jones; Fundi, a joint pseudonym)

PERSONAL: Born Everett LeRoi Jones, October 7, 1934, in Newark, NJ; name changed to Imamu ("spiritual leader") Ameer ("blessed") Baraka ("prince"); later modified to Amiri Baraka; son of Coyette Leroy (a postal worker and elevator operator) and Anna Lois (Russ) Jones; married Hettie Roberta Cohen, October 13, 1958 (divorced, August, 1965); married Sylvia Robinson (Bibi Amina Baraka), 1966; children: (first marriage) Kellie Elisabeth, Lisa Victoria Chapman; (second marriage) Obalaji Malik Ali, Ras Jua Al Aziz, Shani Isis, Amiri Seku, Ahi Mwenge.

Education: Attended Rutgers University, 1951-52; Howard University, B.A., 1954; Columbia University, M.A. (philosophy); New School for Social Research, M.A. (German literature).

ADDRESSES: Office—Department of Africana Studies, State University of New York, Long Island, NY 11794-4340. *Agent*—Joan Brandt, Sterling Lord Literistic, 660 Madison Ave., New York, NY 10021.

CAREER: State University of New York at Stony Brook, assistant professor, 1980-83, associate professor, 1983-85, professor of African studies, 1985—. Instructor, New School for Social Research (now New School University), New York, NY, 1962-64; visiting professor, University of Buffalo, ...

Barber, Karin

© Writers Directory 2005 January 1, 2004

BARBER, Karin. Swedish. Genres: Cultural/Ethnic topics, Language/Linguistics. Career: St. Mary's Teacher Training College, Bukedea, Mbale, Nigeria, teacher, 1967-68; University of Ife, Nigeria, assistant lecturer, 1977-79, lecturer in African languages and literatures, 1979-84; City Literary Institute, London, England, part-time instructor in Yoruba language, 1984-85; University of Birmingham, England, lecturer in West African studies, 1985-93, senior lecturer, 1993-. University of California, Los Angeles, principal instructor in Yoruba, summer, 1982. Institute for Advanced Study and Research in The African Humanities, Northwestern ...

Interview: Lorraine Toussaint and Dante James on the PBS documentary "This Far by Faith"

© NPR Tavis Smiley June 23, 2003
TAVIS SMILEY
Tavis Smiley (NPR)
06-23-2003
Interview: Lorraine Toussaint and Dante James on the PBS documentary "This Far by Faith"

Host: TAVIS SMILEY
Time: 9:00-10:00 AM

TAVIS SMILEY, host:

From NPR in Los Angeles, I'm Tavis Smiley.

(Soundbite of "This Far by Faith")

Ms. LORRAINE TOUSSAINT (Narrator): In the 19th century, Charleston, South Carolina's black community would muster all of its spiritual forces in an effort to bring down the house of bondage with guns, knives and fire, while an enslaved woman in New York would declare herself touched by the breath of God and use her gifts to help make black people free. What was the source ...

Interview: Angelique Kidjo discusses her music

© NPR Tavis Smiley June 17, 2004
TAVIS SMILEY
Tavis Smiley (NPR)
06-17-2004
Interview: Angelique Kidjo discusses her music

Host: TAVIS SMILEY
Time: 9:00-10:00 AM

TAVIS SMILEY, host:

From NPR in Los Angeles, I'm Tavis Smiley.

(Soundbite of song)

Ms. ANGELIQUE KIDJO: (Singing in foreign language)

SMILEY: West African songstress Angelique Kidjo was born in Benin. She sings all kinds of music: African, American, Latin, Caribbean, Brazilian. You name it, she can sing it. She's blessed with a voice that is as charming and as sensual and as powerful as any emerging star on the international scene. Her three Grammy nominations serve as testament to just that. Her ...

Frances Henry. Reclaiming African Religions in Trinidad: the Socio-Political Legitimation of the Orisha and Spiritual Baptist Faiths.(Book Review)

© Latin American Music Review March 22, 2004
FRANCES HENRY. Reclaiming African Religions in Trinidad: The Socio-Political Legitimation of the Orisha and Spiritual Baptist Faiths. Barbados/ Jamaica/ Trinidad and Tobago: The University of the West Indies Press, 2003, 224 pp. Bibliography, photos, glossary, appendix.

My initial reaction on encountering this book was one of enthusiasm, as there have been few recent studies of the Orisha and Spiritual Baptist faiths in the West Indies, and I was already familiar with Henry's work from hearing her lectures during my fieldwork in Trinidad and Tobago (she lives there five months out of the year). I am happy to say that the book did not disappoint me over all, though there are a few areas where I wish the author had provided more detail and analysis.

As Henry states in the preface, she has tried to construct the book so the Orisha community itself can make use of it. Thus, the book is intended more towards that community than towards social ...

African gods came down to earth

© New African November 1, 2012
Back to the Future

At a time of rising religious intolerance on our continent, rather than waste energy on events outside our sphere of influence, it is better that perhaps we think about the things we control - like our attitude to belief. Some of us believe the drama of religion is here on earth.

So what do we believe? At its most basic, do we think that there are truths that only one man can see. That his interpretation of the wonder and drama of the earth is the only version we should follow. And if we do not follow this hegemonic vision of the order things should be on earth - then we should be eternally damned.

Do we believe this approach to truth and the ...

Apples & Oranges?(God Is Not One: The Eight Rival Religions that Run the World--and Why Their Differences Matter)(Book review)

© Commonweal October 8, 2010
God Is Not One
The Eight Rival Religions that Run the World--and Why Their Differences Matter
Stephen Prothero
HarperOne, $26.99, 400 pp.

Stephen Prothero, a professor at Boston University, is fast becoming our national tutor in Religion 101. America's most visible advocate of--and advertisement for--religious literacy, Prothero is both a terrific teacher and a prolific author, one whose erudite but stylish writings are a delight to read. Reading him is like sitting in the class of a brilliant lecturer who dishes out one gleaming felicity after another. We learn, for instance, that when Siddhartha was on the threshold of Awakening and about to become the Buddha, Mara, the demon of sensory pleasure, "sensing trouble ... sent a Bangkok of distractions his way." Or that despite his wife Sita's impeccable fidelity, Rama, the jealous hero of the Hindu epic Ramayana, "apparently has some trust issues." Or that the Buddha himself, cognizant of the power and ambiguity of language, "was forever passing his carefully chosen words through a colander of the useful."

The eight chapters at the heart of Prothero's new book, God Is Not One, lead the reader through what in lesser ...

Lo cubano: Orishas.

© New Internationalist January 1, 2001
A Lo Cubano

by Orishas (Cool Tempo 7243 527082 2 CD)

Rap Cubano! There's a extraordinary verve and sensuality to Don di Niko and Livan (aka Flaco-Pro) and their welding of hip hop, filtered through a Parisian lens and ghetto-raw Havana salsa. Taking their name from the gods of Afro-Latin religion, the two Paris-based producers -- joined by fellow-Orishas and Cuban rappers Roldan, Ruzzo and Yotuel -- have created a debut album that's as fresh as it is timely in its social message.

A Lo Cubano dances a defiant line between salsa and sampling, between the secular and the sacred. From the short opening, with its Yoruba-language priestly incantation, the ...

Feminists born, feminists bred.

© Women and Language March 22, 2003

Abstract: Many Third World women have traditionally had what Western women have recently worked to achieve: autonomy, economic independence, and access to and exercise of power--in cooperation with women and men. These claims are supported by highlighting similar cultural patterns shared by populations on opposite shores of the Atlantic Ocean, in Africa south of the Sahara and Native North America.

Prologue

On Monday July 15, 2002, the Associated Press reported that about 600 unarmed Ijaw women in Escravos, Nigeria had exactly one week earlier taken over the country's largest Chevron-Texaco oil terminal. Holding 700 workers, including Americans, Britons and Canadians hostage, they used walkie talkies to communicate with each other as they negotiated with the oil company. Their threat to strip naked, a culturally-validated practice that irreparably shames the target, in part contributed to their ability to control the facility. "Our weapon is our nakedness," said Helen Odeworitse, a spokeswoman for the group. The women--mainly mothers and wives ages 30 to 90--demanded jobs for their sons, electricity for their homes, and economic development in Nigeria's oil-rich but dirt-poor Niger delta (The Associated Press, Monday July 15, 2002a, p. 14).

Their sons, individually and in ...

GODWIN SADOH: THREE BOOKS

© The Organ March 1, 2008
THE ORGAN WORKS OF FELA SOWANDE: CULTURAL PERSPECTIVES Universe. 110pp. ISBN 978-0-595-47317-5. $US13.95.

INTERCULTURAL DIMENSIONS IN AYO BANKOLE'S MUSIC Universe 132pp. ISBN 978-0-595-46436-4. $US13.95.

JOSHUA UZIOGWE: MEMOIRS OF A NIGERIAN COMPOSER-ETHNOMUSICOLOGIST 135pp. BookSurge Publishing. ISBN 978-1-4196-7380-1.

Godwin Sadoh will be known already to readers of The Organ. He is a Nigerian ethnomusicologist, composer, church musician, organist, pianist, choral conductor and publisher. He is the first African to receive a doctoral degree in organ performance from any institution in the world. He is presently a Professor of Music at Talladega College, Alabama, ...

The charismatic movement in Nigeria today.

© International Bulletin of Missionary Research July 1, 1995
Nigeria, the most populous African nation (98.1 million people, according to mid-1994 estimates), became an independent nation within the British Commonwealth on October 1, 1960. About 49 percent of the country's population is Christian, while Muslims, concentrated in northern Nigeria, account for about 45 percent. Adherents of traditional religion account for the remaining 6 percent.

Sustained Christian mission began in the 1840s, when the Wesleyan Methodist Missionary Society and Church Missionary Society sent missionaries from Sierra Leone and Europe to the southwestern coastal areas. Other missionary societies from Europe and North America came into the country from the late 1840s. Aided by schools and medical work, Christianity was firmly established in southern Nigeria by the late nineteenth century.(1)

A number of major developments have taken place in Nigerian Christianity since the late nineteenth century. Beginning in 1880, there was agitation for more opportunities for African leadership in the churches. In March 1888 this quest resulted in a schism in a Baptist church in Lagos. Other Africans followed the example of the Lagos Baptists and seceded from the Anglican and Methodist churches in 1891, 1901, and 1917. These churches are called ...

From Hierography to Ethnography and Back: Lydia Cabrera's Texts and the Written Tradition in Afro-Cuban Religions

© Journal of American Folklore July 1, 2003

Two common assumptions about Lydia Cabrera's ethnographic work are that it is exclusively the result of fieldwork and that Afro-Cuban religions are based on oral tradition. Evidence is provided in this paper to show that 1) Cabrera also made use of early religious texts as a primary source, and 2) that her work has served as an influence on the texts used in modern Afro-Cuban religious practices, such as the anonymous book Manual del Santero (1990). An analysis is provided of the way in which Cabrera included vernacular written sources in her work, and how her work in turn has become a main source for Santeria "hierography"-the writing about sacred things.

THE RELATIONSHIP BETWEEN ...

COLLEGE DANCE.

(choreographers teach courses around college campuses)(Brief Article)

© Dance Magazine May 1, 1999
Jazz in Russia

Edward R. Truitt, faculty jazz instructor at California State University, Fresno, was invited to St. Petersburg, Russia, to teach a series of jazz technique classes and six composition classes and to give a two-hour lecture: "Jazz Dance in a Historical Context: Past, Present, and Future Trends."

During his stay, January 18 through 23, Truitt's technique class averaged thirty-five dancers; in his composition classes there were twenty-five teachers, choreographers, and students from throughout the country.

"The dancers were highly motivated," says Truitt, "and very eager to learn. It was a great pleasure to teach them. Many of the dancers paid the equivalent of six weeks' salary to attend the one-week workshop."

The workshop week was hosted by Vadim Kasparov and Natasha Kasparov, executive general …

Diaspora and imagined nationality; USA-Africa dialogue and cyberframing Nigerian nationhood.(Brief article)(Book review)

© Reference & Research Book News
April 1, 2012
9781594609268

Diaspora and imagined nationality; USA-Africa dialogue and cyberframing Nigerian nationhood.
Odutola, Koleade.
Carolina Academic Press
2012
176 pages
$30.00
Paperback
African world series
DT515

Odutola (Yoruba language and literature, U. of Florida) examines the on-line information exchange forum founded in 2005 by Toyin Falola (history, U. of Texas). …

Yoruba Proverbs

© Western Folklore January 1, 2009
Yoruba Proverbs. By Oyekan Owomoyela. (Lincoln: University of Nebraska Press, 2005. Pp. xii + 502, acknowledgments, introduction, bibliography. $29.95 paper)

Oyekan Owomoyela's massive collection of over five thousand Yoruba proverbs is the largest of its kind to date and is a major contribution to African proverb study. In the tradition of earlier proverb collections, it is divided into chapters suggesting social themes: "The Good Person," "The Fortunate Person (Or die Good Life)," "Relationships," "Human Nature," "Rights and Responsibilities" and "Truisms." Each proverb is given in Yoruba, followed by an English translation and a brief explanation of the proverb's meaning. The …

ICE HOCKEY

© The World Almanac for Kids 2003
January 1, 2003
The World Almanac for Kids 2003
01-01-2003
ICE HOCKEY

ICE HOCKEY

Ice hockey began in Canada in the mid-1800s. The National Hockey League (NHL) was formed in 1916. In 2002, the NHL had 30 teams⅔24 in the U.S. and 6 in Canada.

In 2001, the Colorado Avalanche won their second Stanley Cup, defeating the defending champion New Jersey Devils 4 games to 3. Colorado goaltender Patrick Roy earned his third Conn Smythe Trophy (Playoff MVP).

Here is a list of Stanley Cup winners since 1990.
1990-91 Season
Winner: Pittsburgh Penguins
Runner-up: Minnesota North Stars
…

Decoding Ignacio Berroa. (PROFILE OF THE MONTH)(Entrevista)

© Latin Beat Magazine April 1, 2007
"The only Latin drummer in the world, in the history of American music that intimately knows both worlds; his native Afro-Cuban music as well as jazz."
--Dizzy Gillespie on Ignacio Berroa.
IGNACIO
"I feel very honored," says Cuban American jazz drummer Ignacio Berroa, talking about his nomination for a Grammy Award this year. "Not too many artists get their first album nominated, and for me, it is quite an accomplishment. People tell me I deserve this because I've paid my dues as a sideman, I do think my past is being factored in by those that vote in the category, but the music speaks for itself."

It was early January and Berroa was packing up his belongings in his Miami home and getting ready to move back to New York City with his wife, Flor Rodríguez, a reporter and TV producer. The longtime sideman with Dizzy Gillespie had now stepped over the line as a bandleader, bringing a refreshing perspective to the national scene at a time when drummers are having a significant presence on the jazz market.

Roy Haynes and the Fountain of Youth Band, …

Baraka, Amiri 1934–

© Concise Major 21st Century Writers
January 1, 2006
(Fundi, a joint pseudonym, Everett LeRoi Jones, LeRoi Jones)

PERSONAL: Born Everett LeRoi Jones, October 7, 1934, in Newark, NJ; name changed to Imamu ("spiritual leader") Ameer ("blessed") Baraka ("prince"); later modified to Amiri Baraka; son of Coyette Leroy (a postal worker and elevator operator) and Anna Lois (Russ) Jones; married Hettie Roberta Cohen, October 13, 1958 (divorced, August, 1965); married Sylvia Robinson (Bibi Amina Baraka), 1966; children: (first marriage) Kellie Elisabeth, Lisa Victoria Chapman; (second marriage) Obalaji Malik Ali, Ras Jua Al Aziz, Shani Isis, Amiri Seku, Ahi Mwenge. *Education:* Attended Rutgers University, 1951–52; Howard University, B.A., 1954; Columbia University, M.A. (philosophy); New School for Social Research, M.A. (German literature).

ADDRESSES: Office—Department of Africana Studies, State University of New York, Long Island, NY 11794-4340. Agent—Joan Brandt, Sterling Lord Literistic, 660 Madison Ave., New York, NY 10021.

CAREER: State University of New York at Stony Brook, assistant professor, 1980–83, associate professor, 1983–85, professor of African studies, 1985–. Instructor, New School for Social Research (now New School University), New York, NY, 1962–64; visiting professor, University of ...

Baraka, Amiri 1934- (Fundi, a joint pseudonym, Everett LeRoi Jones, LeRoi Jones)

© Contemporary Authors, New Revision Series January 1, 2008

PERSONAL:

Born Everett LeRoi Jones, October 7, 1934, in Newark, NJ; name changed to Imamu ("spiritual leader") Ameer ("prince") Baraka ("blessed"); later modified to Amiri Baraka; son of Coyette Leroy (a postal worker and elevator operator) and Anna Lois Jones; married Hettie Roberta Cohen, October 13, 1958 (divorced, August, 1965); married Sylvia Robinson (Bibi Amina Baraka), 1966; children: (first marriage) Kellie Elisabeth, Lisa Victoria Chapman; (second marriage) Obalaji Malik Ali, Ras Jua Al Aziz, Shani Isis, Amiri Seku, Ahi Mwenge. *Ethnicity:* African American. *Education:* Attended Rutgers University, 1951-52; Howard University, B.A., 1954; Columbia University, M.A. (philosophy); New School for Social Research, M.A. (German literature).

ADDRESSES:

Office—Department of Africana Studies, Social and Behavioral Sciences Bldg., Rm. S-249, Stony Brook University, Stony Brook, NY 11794-4340. Agent—Celeste Bateman & Associates, P.O. Box 4071, Newark, NJ 07114-4071.

CAREER:

State University of New York at Stony Brook, assistant professor, 1980-83, associate professor, 1983-85, professor of African studies, 1985—, professor emeritus. New School for Social Research (now ...

Other notes: Bop, Fusion, Blues, World Music, etc.

© Latin Beat Magazine November 1, 1996

The pop-jazz vibe of JOHN MICKIE's debut release Runnin' Out Of Time (Triple Star) consists mostly of Mickie originals and introduces to the "smooth jazz" audience a multi-instrumentalist with a highly melodic sound.

Pianist Niels Lan Doky and bassist Chris Minh Doky may be making their ensemble debut as the DOKY BROTHERS with their selftitled Blue Note Contemporary recording, but the Copenhagen-born siblings of Scandinavian-Vietnamese parentage have been actively involved in jazz circles for years. Working with their own compositions as well as covers, the Doky Brothers find the perfect balance between the strong melodic lines and the freedom to improvise.

Tenor saxophonist JOVON JACKSON is as comfortable with the blues as he is stretching out on advanced harmonies, as demonstrated on the CD A Look Within (Blue Note), where he continues to widen the repertoire and experiment ...

Religion in the Age of Transformation.(Review)

© Social Forces September 1, 1999

Edited by Madeleine Cousineau. Praeger Publishers, 1998. xv + 235 pp. Cloth, $65.00; paper, $22.95.

Reviewer: KEVIN J. CHRISTIANO, University of Notre Dame

Madeleine Cousineau has set out to accomplish a difficult task with this new set of original readings for the sociology of religion. Specialists in the study of South America already know her for the several monographs that she has authored on the internal dynamics of the Catholic Church in Brazil. Others doubtless are aware of her activities in the promotion of improvements to teaching through publication of syllabi and instructional materials for the Teaching Resources Center of the American Sociological ...

Yoruba indigenous knowledges in the African Diaspora: knowledge, power and the politics of indigenous spirituality. (Dissertation Abstracts: JPAS 2011 Selections)(Report)(Author abstract)

© Journal of Pan African Studies March 1, 2012

This study investigates how Yoruba migrants make meaning of Yoruba Indigenous knowledges in the African Diaspora, specifically within the geopolitical space of dominant Canadian culture. This research is informed by the lived experiences of 16 Africans of Yoruba descent now living in Toronto, Canada, and explores how these first and second generation migrants construct the spiritual and linguistic dimensions of Yoruba Indigenous identities in their everyday lives. While Canada is often imagined as a sanctuary for progressive politics, it nonetheless is also a hegemonic space where inequities continue to shape the social engagements of everyday life. Hence, this dissertation situates the ...

Family ties.(NEW YORK NOTEBOOK)(Alvin Ailey American Dance Theater)(Brief Article)

© Dance Magazine December 1, 2005

To Ronald K. Brown, the Alvin Ailey American Dance Theater counts as an adopted family. The works he's choreographed for them, like Sen, ins Nia and Grace, reveal a blood-thick fondness. "Each time I come to Ailey, I feel that I can go deeper, I can ask more from the dancers," says Brown. His newest ballet, which the company premieres on Dec. 7, is titled Ife/My Heart. ...

On the Side of My People: A Religious Life of Malcolm X.

© The Historian March 22, 1998

On the Side of My People. A Religious Life Of Malcolm X. By Louis A. DeCaro Jr. (New York and London: New York University Press, 1996. Pp. 361. $29.95.)

This is probably the most definitive work to date on the controversial but celebrated civil rights advocate. Louis DeCaro is a skillful researcher and deserves the commendation of anyone who is interested in comprehending the phenomenal transformation of Malcolm X from a dope dealer, thug, and hustler to a major African American civil-rights leader. DeCaro discusses some familiar events in the life of Malcolm, including his difficult early childhood, his dose relationship to his parents, life in the streets, and conversion to the Nation of Islam (NOI). Also covered in detail is the pervasiveness of racism and discrimination in America at the turn of the century, including an analysis of the social ramifications of the influx of African Americans to ...

Beyond Fela and Ade

© The Stranger April 6, 2006
Beyond Fela and Ade

African Comps Dig for Gold by Andy Beta

AS A RELATIVE newcomer to African music's multifarious pleasures, I find it hard to overcome the images of the continent scorched into my head of drought, blight, and famine thanks to heartrending video montages I saw in the '80s. While I once believed Africa to be but dust and flies, the opening lick from juju master Ebenezer Obey on Lagos All Routes suggests otherwise. Expansive and deep, shimmering yet powerful, Obey's liquid guitar tone on the 10-minute "Eyi Yato/Elere 3Ni Wa" evokes nothing less than the mightiest river. And so it follows that the rest of these two compilations of Nigerian Afropop overflow with ...

Report from interreligious consultation on "Conversion--Assessing the Reality": Lariano (Italy): May 12-16, 2006.

© International Review of Mission July 1, 2007

Introduction

We, the participants in the inter-faith reflection on "Conversion: Assessing the Reality", met at Lariano (Italy) on May 12-16, 2006. We, 27 of us, belong to Buddhism, Christianity, Hinduism, Islam, Judaism and Yoruba religion. We shared our views and experiences on this important subject over five days of co-living in the peaceful, idyllic and spiritually vibrant surroundings of Villa Mater Dei--a kind of inter-faith pilgrimage, brief but fulfilling. Our deliberations were intense, and took place in an atmosphere of cordiality, mutual respect and commitment to learn from one another's spiritual heritage, which together constitute the common inheritance of the entire humankind.

We affirm our commitment to the process of inter-religious dialogue. Its necessity and usefulness have increased exponentially in our times for promoting peace, harmony and conflict-transformation--within and among nations in our ...

Empowering African languages: rethinking the strategies.(Report)

© Journal of Pan African Studies March 15, 2008

Introduction

As a budding scholar in linguistic studies, I have attended some conferences whose themes addressed the vexed issue of the marginalisation of African languages and the imperative need to develop and empower them. Apart from such attendances at conferences, I have also read articles written by experts in linguistics and the central issue has been that African languages are endangered due to the hegemonic influence of either English or French. Having followed this issue with very keen interest, I would like to take a retrospective look, at this juncture, to assess the journey so far and reflect on the essence of the 'Save African Languages Project'. This is with a view to ascertaining how close (preferably) we are to the African linguistics of our dream or how far (regrettably) we are from it.

Each time I scan the articles related to this issue in question, I get excited at some lofty proposals, suggestions and resolutions put forward by scholars as to how African languages can be empowered to meet the challenges of development processes. Consequently, I have come to appreciate the passion for the utilization of African indigenous languages as veritable tools for the development of African communities. But ...

Seven.

© New Internationalist September 1, 1997

(Virgin 724384281625 CD)

The first thing that strikes you about `Jogging a Tombouctou' - the opening number to Zap Mama's third album - is its sheer speed. Half-singing, half rapping, Marie Daulne, the band's leader, fairly fires the French words out and it's only a few seconds later that the melodies or the sing-song rhythms of the music actually grab the attention. It is a typical Zap Mama tactic. Now in their seventh year, Zap Mama have specialized in making the sort of first impressions that ensure listeners return for more. With a music drawing from influences which mix James Brown with sounds from Daulne's upbringing (and subsequent flight) from the former Belgian Congo, ...

REFLECTIONS AFTER SEEING AMISTAD

© Peacework January 1, 1998
Reginald L. Jackson, visual anthropologist who has taught communications at Simmons College, is founder of the Boston-area Olaleye Communications, Inc.

A people without a culture is a people without a past. A people without a past is a people without a future.

--Dr. Wande Abimbola

Make no mistake about it. The power of the movie Amistad is of epic proportions. The first frames project lightning and thunder, making immediate contact with natural forces that need to be reconciled. (The Yoruba of southwestern Nigeria believe in the divinity of nature and the need to appease natural forces through sacrifice in order to maintain a balanced way of life. The deities Sango

...

Hot tickets: A preview of the 2001-02 cultural season--plus some picks of our own

© New Orleans Magazine September 1, 2001

NEW ORLEANS OPERA ASSOCIATION Theatre of the Performing Arts, 801 N. Rampart St., 529-3000.

THE SEASON: "Faust" (Oct. 11 and 13), "Die Walkure" ("The Valkyrie") (Nov. 15 and 17), "Turandot" (March 7 and 9) and "Porgy and Bess" (April 11 and 13).

HOT TICKIT: NOOA's 59th season is spectacular, with returning masterpieces not seen in more than a decade and the New Orleans debut of Gershwin's "Porgy and Bess." The standout in this stellar season is "Die Walkure" ("The Valkyrie"), Wagner's most famous opera in his "Ring Cycle." With some of the most popular and famous music written for opera, "Die Walkure" transports the viewer to a mystical world in which gods and goddesses, ...

The mediated production of ethnicity and nationalism among the Iban of Sarawak, 1954-1976 (1). (Research Notes).(Malaysia)

© Borneo Research Bulletin January 1, 2001

Introduction

Among the recent deluge of anthropological writings on ethnicity (see Levine 1999), J. Comaroff's (1996) essay Ethnicity, Nationalism, and the Politics of Difference in an Age of Revolution stands as a model of clarity and eloquence. Comaroff sets out to investigate the contemporary upsurge in the world's "politics of identity." Why are the politics of cultural identity back with a vengeance when modernity was supposed to erase all differences of origin? he asks. His answer is twofold. First, the theoretical discussions of the past two decades are no reliable guide to a proper inquiry. Ethnicity theorists are still caught up in a fruitless dichotomy: primordialism versus constructionism. Primordialists assert that all peoples have a "primordial" attachment to place, kin and/or language (see Karlsson 1998: 136). "How many more times," asks Comaroff (1996: 164), "is it necessary to prove that all ethnic identities are historical creations before primordialism is consigned, finally, to the trash heap of ideas past?" Most social anthropologists today reject this approach and opt for constructivism, yet, to Comaroff (1996: 165), constructivism is not a theory but "merely a broad ...

New York Glory: Religions in the City & Public Religion and Urban Transformation: Faith in the City. .(Book Review)

© Sociology of Religion March 22, 2003

New York Glory: Religions in the City, TONY CARNES and ANNA KARPATHAKIS (eds.). New York & London: New York University Press, 2001. xvi + 440 pp., $60.00 (cloth), $19.50 (paper). and Public Religion and Urban Transformation: Faith in the City, LOWELL LIVEZEY (ed.). New York and London: New York University Press, 2000, xiv + 364pp., $65.00 (cloth), $19.00 (paper).

These two edited volumes bring together a variety of authors to offer a rare combination: they focus on religion in urban America and on particular cities, namely New York City and Chicago. In addition, each attempts to give an overview of the dynamism and variety of contemporary religious institutions and expressions in these cities, not concentrating on a delimited part of the city, subgroup, or subtype of religion. It is the contemporary broader role of religion in these cities that is at issue. As such, they make no claims about religion in other cities nor directly about urban American religion more generally. That said, the two volumes are also very different in how they go about their task, being informed by different strategies and different purposes.

Capturing all the complex ...

...

A Samba for Sherlock

© Americas (English Edition) March 1, 1999

A Samba for Sherlock [O Xango de Baker Street], by Jo Soares. Trans., Clifford E. Landers. New York: Vintage International, 1998.

If you think you know Sherlock Holmes, think again. Brazilian writer Jo Soares recasts Conan Doyle's reserved, pipe-smoking detective as a bungler in the tropics. Set in Rio de Janeiro in 1886, the story revolves around the theft of a Stradivarius violin and a series of murders. The emperor Dom Pedro has given the valuable instrument to his favorite mistress, Maria Luisa. Shortly after it disappears, a mysterious killer begins to prey on young women. The corpses of his victims-a common prostitute, a lady-in-waiting, a charity worker, and finally, Maria ...

SALVADOR DA BAHIA A TRULY AFRICAN CITY

© New African January 1, 2004

Salvador da Bahia is the capital of Bahia, a state in northeast Brazil which is larger than France, and the most African of all the Brazilian states. Simon Dungworth has been there to meet with the long-lost African brethren. This is his report.

Anyone thinking about carnival in Brazil usually has the image of Rio's extravagant affair with hundreds of amazing floats followed by thousands of samba dancers, singers, and drummers. But there is a city in Brazil that hosts one of the most exciting carnivals in the world, a city that is immensely proud of its African culture and heritage. It is called Salvador da Bahia, the capital of the Bahia state, and situated in northeast ...

Toyin Falola and Ann Genova (eds), Yoruba Identity and Power Politics.(Book review)

© Africa March 22, 2008

TOYIN FALOLA AND ANN GENOVA (eds), Yoruba Identity and Power Politics. Rochester NY: University of Rochester Press (hb 45.00 [pounds sterling]/$75.00--978 15804 6219 8). 2006, 384 pp.

Without Toyin Falola, the state of

Nigerian and especially Yoruba studies would not be what it is. Publishing at least a book per year and usually more, Falola is of fabled productivity. Recently, the first volume of Falola's autobiography, A Mouth Sweeter than Salt (2004), was critically acclaimed and it is, along with Wole Soyinka's Ake, one of the most appealing books on a Yoruba childhood I have read. As most of Falola's books are edited volumes, his contribution to the subject goes beyond his own person and often involves the promotion of the academic careers of younger scholars, both from Nigeria and beyond. His co-editor Ann Genova, currently a PhD student at the University of Texas, has already collaborated with Falola on two books in 2005.

This book is timely and reflects the variety of new ...

Drama: Drama and Religion

© Encyclopedia of Religion January 1, 2005

Although it can be said that the presentation of drama and religious ceremony are analogous, the two practices are not always directly related in world history. The notion popularized in the early twentieth century by the Cambridge School that drama springs directly from ritual has been largely discredited. However, religious practices and dramatic presentation often share many common elements: costume, storytelling, a playing space, and an audience. Also many of the world's dramatic forms are derived from religious rituals and are still, in some way, connected to religious celebration. With that in mind, drama has had a long, sometimes intimate, sometimes adversarial relationship with religion.

Scholars generally assign drama and religious ritual to a continuum with the following divisions: ritual with performative elements, ritual drama, drama presented as part of a religious festival, and secular drama. While this continuum cannot be used as a trajectory of theatrical development, it provides a useful tool with which to understand the many kinds of relationships theatrical performance has had with religious practice. Some societies developed rituals with advanced elements of performance but never developed anything approaching a secular drama. Conversely, some societies adopted a secular ...

Dom Obá II D'África

© Encyclopedia of African-American Culture and History January 1, 2006
c. 1845
July 8, 1890

The popular Afro-Brazilian leader Dom Obá II D'África was born Cândido da Fonseca Galvão, in Lençóis, in the interior of the then province of Bahia. Dom Obá was the son of a freed African slave. He was also an African prince, thought to be the grandson of Aláàfin Abiodun, the founder of the Yoruba Empire.

A warrior prince, Dom Obá was a volunteer with the Brazilian forces in the Paraguayan War (1865–1870). In recognition of his bravery, he was made an honorary officer in the army. After being demobilized, Dom Obá settled in Rio de ...

Myal

© Encyclopedia of African-American Culture and History January 1, 2006

Myal was an African-Jamaican form of divination and a ritual dance by which spirit mediums drew on the power of ancestors to heal and to alleviate misfortune ascribed to the jealousy, greed, and enmity of others. Obeah, another type of divination, inspired terror during periods of insecurity when people believed that evil Obeah specialists endangered them. To counteract the danger, they called on Myal mediums.

Even before leaving Africa as slaves, Africans associated malevolent sorcery with enslavement, devising fantastic symbolic tales and rumors about slave trafficking and slavery that acted as a critique of African and European slavers and slave owners. These tales described slave dealers and owners as cannibals or vampires who consumed African flesh and blood and processed them ...

Nigeria

© Governments of the World: A Global Guide to Citizens' Rights and Responsibilities January 1, 2006

Nigeria is a federal republic consisting of thirty-six states and a federal capital located in Abuja. The country lies on the west coast of the African continent and has a land mass of 923,768 square kilometers (356,700 square miles), making it slightly larger than California. It is bordered to the north by the Republic of Niger, to the south by the Atlantic Ocean, to the east by the Federal Republic of Cameroon, and to the west by the Republic of Benin. On the country's northeast border is Lake Chad, which also extends into the Republic of Niger and Chad and touches the northernmost part of Cameroon. Nigeria's location between the equator and Tropics of Cancer places it entirely within the tropical zone, but climatic conditions vary from equatorial on the coast, to tropical in the middle, to arid in the north.

The World Bank estimated Nigeria's population in 1990 at 119 million with an estimated annual growth rate of 3.3 percent, making the country the most populated state in Africa and the tenth most populated nation in the world. Although Nigeria's population is comprised of over 250 ethnic groups, three major ethnic groups account for over 66 percent of the total population and primarily reside in three geographical regions: the Hausa/Fulani in the ...

Indigenous Organizations and Development.

© Journal of Development Studies June 1, 1997

This collection explores what the editors Peter Blunt and Michael Warren call the 1980s 'paradigm shift' in development thinking which stressed 'participation in ... decision-making by the clientele group, [and] building the capacity of individuals and institutions in the development process' ('Introduction', p.xiii). This shift led to increasing interest in development circles on understanding, and taking into account, the point of view of the supposed beneficiaries, and a concern with 'the nature of indigenous or local-level community-based knowledge and how it provided the basis for both individual and community-level decision-making' (ibid). The focus of the present volume is indigenous organisations and the part that they can and do play in 'development'. There is a 'Preface' by Norman Uphoff, a very short 'Introduction' by Blunt; and Warren, and 20 papers grouped by region: nine on Africa (five on the Yoruba), four on the Indian subcontinent, and seven on 'Asia-Pacific', a region including Canada and ...

Mark Lotz & Shango's Dance: Cuban Fishes Make Good Dishes. (Reseña de audio grabación)

© Latin Beat Magazine February 1, 2005
MARK LOTZ & SHANGO'S DANCE Cuban Fishes Make Good Dishes (Random Chance)

Flutist Mark Lotz (from the Netherlands) and friends come together with several Cuban musicians to from the ensemble Shango's Dance. The recording marks the third production by the ensemble aimed at documenting its European interpretations of santería music. Fourteen tracks display a crossover of Afro-Cuban religious folklore with jazz idioms and other popular forms. Recorded in the Netherlands and Cuba, Shango's Dance captures the various rhythms, which are a part of the ...

In Cuba, Baha'is celebrate a renovation.(CELEBRATION)

© One Country April 1, 2005
HAVANA, Cuba -- Government officials and representatives of diverse religious groups in Cuba gathered with Baha'is in May to celebrate the opening of a newly reconstructed Baha'i Center here.

First acquired in 1956, the central Havana Center had recently been completely rebuilt, and the 23 May 2005 celebration was held to open it to other religious communities.

In attendance were not only representatives from the Jewish, Christian, Muslim, and African Yoruba religious communities but also Caridad Diego Bello, the chief of religious affairs in the Cuban government, and two other officials from her office.

Ms. Diego expressed her gratitude to the ...

Carlos "Go Go" Gomez. (Homenaje al asmatico)(Reseña de audio grabación)

© Latin Beat Magazine March 1, 2006
CARLOS "GO GO" GOMEZ Homenaje Al Asmatico (In Homage to the Asthmatic One) (Kidlat Records)

Born to Cuban and Puerto Rican parents in the Bronx, New York City, Carlos Gómez first began playing Latin percussion professionally at age 14. He was a member of the group Seguida (a pioneering seventies Latin rock band from New York City that experimented with the fusion of Latin rhythms, salsa and rock & roll). After a decade of playing and studying ethnomusicology at the City College of New York, Gómez headed west to California to continue his musical career and studies of spirituality and religion. Settling in the San Francisco Bay area he worked with jazz luminaries such ...

Female circumcision and other dangerous practices to women's health. (in Nigeria) (Transcript)

© WIN News June 22, 1993
"The majority, if not all, of the dangerous practices which are harmful to maternal health in Nigeria are performed under the auspices of traditional or cultural beliefs and inclinations. . . It is an established fact that the more severe the effect of any of the harmful practices the more likely it is that the victim will be either women or children. . ."

"Female circumcision (FC) in general terms can be described as a traditional practice in which a person, sometimes unskilled or a health worker, cuts off parts or whole organs of the female external genitalia. . . It is deeply tied to cultural and traditional beliefs. . ."

"A national survey by ...

Ignacio Berroa: Codes.(Reseña de audio grabación)

© Latin Beat Magazine August 1, 2006
IGNACIO BERROA Codes (Blue Note)

On Codes, his first album as a leader, drummer Ignacio Berroa delivers an introspective Latin jazz offering that glows with provocative music and talented players. Renowned as a sideman with luminaries like jazz icon Dizzy Gillespie and Cuban pianist Gonzalo Rubalcaba, Berroa leads much as Art Blakey did; he never hampers the musicians and lets them shape the themes with stellar ensemble and improvisational skill. Allowing the interplay to foster, Ignacio then compliments the proceedings with an orchestral sense of coloration and drive. The Chick Corea composition Matrix, with David Sánchez on tenor sax, serves as the gateway to seven ...

Resources for Teaching "Women and Religion": Five Readers. (Book Reviews).(Bibliography)

© Feminist Collections: A Quarterly of Women's Studies Resources January 1, 2003
Elizabeth A. Castelli, ed., with Rosamond C. Rodman, WOMEN, GENDER, RELIGION' A READER. NewYork: Palgrave, 2001. 550p. bibl. $89.95, ISBN 0-312-24004-X; pap., $27.95, ISBN 0-312-24030-9.

Nancy Auer Falk & Rita M. Gross, eds., UNSPOKEN WORLDS: WOMEN'S RELIGIOUS LIVES. Belmont, CA: Wadsworth, 2000 (3rd ed). 310p. bibl. ill, pap., $43.95, ISBN 0-534-51570-3.

Darlene M. Juschka, ed., FEMINISM IN THE STUDY OF RELIGION: A READER. London & New York: Continuum, 2000 (cloth), 2001 (pap.). c593p. bibl. index. $107.95, ISBN 0826-4-4726-0; pap., $29.95, ISBN 0-8264-4727-9.

Nancy Nason-Clark & Mary Jo Neitz, eds., FFMINIST NARRATIVES AND THE SOCIOLOGY OF RELIGION Walnut Creek, CA: AltaMira, 2001. 141p. bibl. $59.00, ISBN 0-7591-0197-3; pap., $19.95, ISBN 0-7591-0198-1.

Lucinda Joy Peach, WOMEN AND WORLD RELIGIONS. Upper Saddle River, NJ: Prentice Hall, 2002. 394p. bibl. index, pap., $36.20, ISBN 0-13-

040444-6.

In preparing to write this essay, I surveyed a number of syllabi for undergraduate courses in "Women and Religion" from a variety of colleges and universities. I wanted to see how others teaching these courses understand the subject and what ...

Lagos - Brooklyn - Brixton.

© New Internationalist September 1, 1997
(Triple Earth TECD 116 CD)

The first thing that strikes you about 'Jogging a Tombouctou' - the opening number to Zap Mama's third album - is its sheer speed. Half-singing, half rapping, Marie Daulne, the band's leader, fairly fires the French words out and it's only a few seconds later that the melodies or the sing-song rhythms of the music actually grab the attention. It is a typical Zap Mama tactic. Now in their seventh year, Zap Mama have specialized in making the sort of first impressions that ensure listeners return for more. With a music drawing from influences which mix James Brown with sounds from Daulne's upbringing (and subsequent flight) from the former Belgian ...

Black Puerto Rican Identity and Religious Experience

© The Catholic Historical Review July 1, 2007
Black Puerto Rican Identity and Religious Experience. By Samiri Herández Hiraldo. [New Directions in Puerto Rican Studies.] (GainesvUle: The University Press of Florida. 2006. Pp. xxii, 292. $55.00.)

Through Dr. Hernández Hiraldo's investigation we are able to enter a world that is known mainly for its religious African folklore. A serious anthropological research on the multidimensional religious experience of the Loizans has never been accomplished untU this field study was made. What we find here is kind of top secret and very revealing of this community's ups and downs. Through almost an entire year of field word, the author not only shows us that Loizans are spiritists (or ...

Yoruba in Diaspora: An African Church in London

© African Studies Review April 1, 2008
Hermione Harris. Yoruba in Diaspora: An African Church in London. New York: Palgrave Macmillan, 2006. vii + 294 pp. Charts. Glossary. Notes. Bibliography. Index. $69.95. Cloth.

This is a remarkable book for two reasons. First, because it was written fully thirty-five years after the initial research started, in 1969, to be resumed only in the 1990s. Second, because the book stands out for its sensitive discussion of an important but often neglected dimension of African religiosity, namely spiritual power. This is discussed through a case study of the Cherubim and Seraphim Church in London, as founded by Nigerian immigrants in the 1960s.

The issue of spiritual power runs as ...

Religion in the Contemporary South: Diversity, Community, and Identity.

© Sociology of Religion March 22, 1996

Observers of southern culture are finding that the equation of southern culture with white evangelical Protestantism is no longer descriptive of contemporary southern religion. Increasing urbanization and population shifts not only introduce new expressions but shape the contours of groups already in place. This volume aids understanding of the variety of sources that fashion and maintain religious identity in the context of southern culture.

One approach to understanding how hegemony operates is to look at those sites in which resistance takes place. The Baptist-Methodist dominance in the Old South faces change and challenge. These authors, primarily anthropologists, document the diversity of alternate religious identities in the South, and the ways in which they oppose and adapt to longstanding as well as emerging, "New South," beliefs ...

Sola Akingbola: Routes to Roots: Yoruba Drums From Nigeria.

(Sound recording review)(Brief article)
© Sing Out! June 22, 2008
SOLA AKINGBOLA
Routes to Roots:
Yoruba Drums From Nigeria
Are Music 2114

While his name is more known for tastefully accompanying UK-based funk/soul outfit Jamiroquai, Nigerian native Sola Akingbola derives his mastery of rhythm from more homegrown influences: Fela Kuti, King Sunny Ade and Manu Dibango. His Yoruba heritage has offered him an inside track to an exceptional career governed by sound--the Orishas, or deities, are manifestations of the Great Spirit. They are appeased by offerings of music; in fact, they are manifestations of music. This makes Yoruba music devotional by default, a quality Akingbohi would have no problem ...

Long John Oliva's AC Jazz Project.(Resena de audio grabacion)

© Latin Beat Magazine April 1, 2003
Lucumi (Orishas Records)

This new CD by percussionist/bandleader Long John Oliva and the AC Jazz Project displays the percussive talents of this Havanese master drummer--Oliva was raised in Belén, home of the traditional Afro-Cuban rumba. Taught by his father and master drummer Pancho Quinto, Oliva followed in the steps and styles of master percussionists Carlos "El Niño" Alfonso, Tata Güines and José Luis "Changuito" Quintana. Proficient at playing rumba as well as jazz or world rhythms, Oliva and crew unveil a repertoire of cutting edge ...

Desde La Bahia--San Francisco. (Columna)

© Latin Beat Magazine October 1, 2002
ALBITA: When Cuban singer-songwriter Albita Rodríguez arrived in the U.S. in 1993, she splashed onto the Miami, Florida scene with a look and sound described as "part Marlene Dietrich and part Benny Moré." Creating a brand of salsa with producer Emilio Estefan that drew inspiration from the

folkloric guajiro music of her native country and a fusion of American and Latin pop influences, she landed on the Billboard charts with the albums No Se Parece A Nada and Una Mujer Como Yo.

Her three recordings on Emilio Estefan's Crescent Moon/Epic label put her on the map as one of the leading Latina voices of the 1990s. A few years ago she began to take a more active role as a producer and the Sony-owned label dropped her when they didn't accept her album Son for release. She took some financial lumps but landed with Times Square Records in New York City. That label released Son and her latest effort, Hecho a Mano (Made By Hand).

"Sony didn't like the last album I offered them," remembers Albita from her home in Southern Florida recently. "Every day the business side gets more difficult for artists. There area lot of intermediaries between the public and performers. In many cases you rely on people who don't even know what they're selling. That's not the worst, ...

Varios artistas y videos.(TT: VARIOUS ARTISTS AND VIDEOS.)(Artículo Breve)

© Latin Beat Magazine October 1, 2001 (Orisha Productions)

Today's high-tech satellite communications systems can bring hundreds of television signals, movie channels, sports channels and music video channels into a person's home, regardless of their location on the globe. Music video channels like MTV and VH1 are being broadcast in some areas in Spanish to attract more Hispanic viewers. Puma TV from Venezuela is a Spanish video channel dedicated primarily to Latin music but also airs mainstream contemporary English videos as well. Joining Spanish networks, top video shows such as Control and Caliente (whose target audience ranges from 12-22 years old) are HBO Latino's music video programs, featuring top ...